Great food should look beautiful, taste special, and make you feel good.

In *Bright Cooking*, her highly anticipated first cookbook, celebrated chef and tastemaker Camille Becerra offers 140+ fresh, natural recipes to boost one's mood with stunning beauty and one's body with vegetable-forward, healthful ingredients. More than 90 foundational pantry basics—modern mother sauces, broths, dusts, finishing oils, and more—are combined in uncommon and uncomplicated ways to create 50+ eat-anytime dishes.

Say you went to the farmers' market and bought some beautiful chicories. From there, you could add some Chile-Mushroom Pickle to create Maple Chicories with Chile-Mushroom Pickle Toast. Maybe you're not in the mood to put together an involved meal, but you picked up some squash at the market—you could char it and nestle it in a cloud of Fennel Pollen Yogurt with a dusting of pistachios for a thrown-together treat, or add Coconut-Ginger Broth and curry paste to create a warming, brothy bowl.

Bright Cooking inspires you to create based on what you have in your kitchen, what you hunger for, and what your body is asking for. With advice throughout on adding big flavor and playfulness to your repertoire, *Bright Cooking* is a uniquely beautiful primer that teaches home cooks new ways of cooking and thinking about nourishing, flavorful food. After you work your way through the book, you'll only be a smear of this, a few sprinkles of that, and a flourish away from confidence and creative freedom in the kitchen—and you'll feel amazing, inside and out.

BRIGHT
COOKING

BRIGHT

Recipes for the Modern Palate

CAMILLE BECERRA

COOKING

CHRONICLE BOOKS

SAN FRANCISCO

Library of Congress Cataloging-in-Publication Data

Names: Becerra, Camille, author.
Title: Bright cooking : recipes for the modern palate / Camille Becerra.
Description: San Francisco : Chronicle Books, [2024] | Includes index.
Identifiers: LCCN 2023059025 | ISBN 9781797213859 (hardcover)
Subjects: LCSH: Cooking (Natural foods) | Pescatarian cooking. | LCGFT: Cookbooks.
Classification: LCC TX741 .B424 2024 | DDC 641.5/637–dc23/eng/20240102
LC record available at https://lccn.loc.gov/2023059025

Manufactured in China.

MIX
Paper | Supporting responsible forestry
FSC™ C104723
www.fsc.org

Food styling by Camille Becerra.
Design by Vanessa Dina.
Typesetting by Frank Brayton.

Some of the recipes in this book include raw eggs and seafood. Consumed raw, these foods pose a risk for bacteria that are killed by proper cooking. Please purchase from trusted sources and follow recipe instructions carefully.

10 9 8 7 6 5 4 3 2 1

Chronicle books and gifts are available at special quantity discounts to corporations, professional associations, literacy programs, and other organizations. For details and discount information, please contact our premiums department at corporatesales@chroniclebooks.com or at 1-800-759-0190.

Chronicle Books LLC
680 Second Street
San Francisco, California 94107
www.chroniclebooks.com

I
ELEMENTS

II

DISHES

I've always been enamored with vegetables and fruits. When I was growing up, my mom would buy a bag of peaches in the summer, and I would eat them all in a single afternoon, tasting each of them in search of the deep ambrosial flavor. I remember having a very sensitive palate from an early age, and I could easily distinguish delicate flavors that others couldn't. I never liked eating processed foods because I thought they all tasted synthetic, and that flavor was off-putting to me. I want this book to help you tap into your own senses and the way you take time to taste and to encourage you to question the products you're putting into your bodies. My body has always guided me toward delicious, healthful foods.

I grew up in a Puerto Rican household in Elizabeth, New Jersey, a melting pot of different cultures, and I got to experience a lot of varied cuisines while eating at friends' homes. In my teens, someone gave me the *Moosewood Cookbook*, a vegetarian cookbook that allowed me to travel the world through its pages. I was obsessed with this handwritten book and read through it as if it were a thriller. Cooking techniques, ingredients I hadn't heard of before, and the lifestyle that spoke through the book were fascinating and exciting! Before then, I didn't know what vegetarian cuisine was. It was that book and lessons from my mother and an aunt, both exceptional cooks who transferred valuable generational recipes to me, that led me to lean into a life in food.

After graduating high school, I took a gap year and traveled across the United States. I spent time in areas where there was more of a focus on celebrating beautiful ingredients, eating well, and farming. From there I gravitated toward technique and was drawn to both the process and the experience of cooking, especially the social connection of food—how it brought people together around the table. These experiences fed a seedling of an idea to create a career in food for myself. But it wasn't without risk; my mom, who grew up in the mountains of Puerto Rico, believed that to be successful, you had to go to college and find a legitimate career. For her, being in the kitchen was grueling hard work without reward, and being a chef wasn't a viable career choice. But that didn't stop the somewhat gravitational pull of a newly built little culinary school in southern New Jersey by the ocean that had brought in French chefs to teach. In the summer, when I wasn't taking classes, I would work in little restaurants by the beach like the Washington Inn, the nicest restaurant in Cape May. I developed my knife skills by slicing boxes of cucumbers and sacks of onions by hand for their famous bread-and-butter pickles that were placed on each table with bread service.

When I graduated, I moved to Philadelphia, the closest major city to the school. I took a job at the first place that hired me, a vegetarian restaurant. Vegetarian restaurants at that time were very community based, and there I met a chef who taught me about macrobiotic cuisine. His knowledge helped me appreciate another layer of the history and medicinal aspects of food. That's where I began to understand that food has the ability to cure.

My wanderlust kicked in just as this chef told me about a retreat center looking for a cook. I got a one-way ticket to New Mexico and arrived at what was a Zen center. They hosted retreats as a source of revenue and needed cooks, and they encouraged all the employees to join their practice every day. With zero knowledge of Zen Buddhism, I began the meditation practice I maintain to this day.

It was at this Zen center where I truly learned how to cook. A Zen nun kept a huge, well-rounded garden on the grounds with vegetables, grains, and flowers. Everything we prepared was vegetarian per Buddhist practice, so we made tofu, yogurt, vinegar, granola, and the like. This environment helped me further understand how to grow and cook food—how the act of cooking and eating is deeply meditative and rooted in resourcefulness. I remember in that experience really understanding that food should be simple . . . the simpler, the better. When it is, the quality of the ingredients has a beautiful platform to shine. This experience made me realize that I had a greater mission in life, and cooking was how I would make a difference. I knew the world would be a better place if everyone knew how and what to cook to nourish their fullest selves.

After the Zen center, I moved to New York City. I felt like a somewhat trained chef and was set on going big, which meant working at the four-star restaurant of the time, Le Cirque 2000. I applied; they said no. This happened time and time again with the other leading restaurants.

I didn't realize it at the time, but women didn't work in those kitchens. Ultimately, the people who did finally hire me were from female-owned and -led restaurants and kitchens, many of which, funnily enough, were vegetarian, vegan, or macrobiotic. This was a blessing in disguise—it helped provide more ground for the foundation of the vegetable-forward food I am known for today.

Still, I yearned to do something fancy and very much wanted to go into fine dining. I also knew I would eventually want to own a restaurant, and I needed experience in all aspects of the business, including front of house. Through my friendship with another young woman from New Jersey who was creating beautiful spaces and redefining the industry in an inspiring way, I became familiar with the restaurant hospitality and nightlife scene and the many people who contribute to it: the DJs, maître d's, promoters, bartenders, door people, etc. Working with these amazing people helped me understand the energy between the front of the house and the kitchen and how they are essential for a restaurant's success. I also realized that dining is about a full experience: great food plus a great environment.

After 9/11, my young daughter and I were forced to move from Tribeca to Greenpoint, Brooklyn, where a thriving Polish community, some Puerto Ricans, and a sprinkling of artists lived. At that time, it was a culinary desert. You could get good kielbasa but nothing else. At this point, I had worked in every position of a restaurant and I was ready to put what I'd learned into practice. I opened my first restaurant there and named it Paloma, after my daughter. I wanted Paloma to be a neighborhood spot, a little more elevated than burgers and fries.

In 2006, in the middle of the night, I received a call from one of my dearest friends, Errickson Wilcox, a doorman at the famous club Marquis. He said, "You won't believe this, but the people from *Top Chef* came in, and they're looking for chefs." I was not big on TV, so I had never heard of *Top Chef*, but it seemed like a great opportunity, so I dashed to Manhattan to audition. Less than a month later, I was filming Season 3 in Miami. Streaming old episodes online wasn't a thing back then, so I had no idea what I was getting myself into. I remember the opening scene was shot at the Versace mansion in Miami. None of the contestants had met yet. Suddenly, we all stepped out of our cars, and I was like, "Whoa, where did they find all these cool people?" It felt like an MTV reality show. And just like that, food got really hip. Although the experience ultimately wasn't for me, it was a life-changing time with such a great group of talented chefs.

In 2009, deep into the recession, we had a fire at Paloma. A month later, my landlord decided to serve me papers and evict me. I felt we were being kicked when we were down. I decided to move back to Manhattan soon after. Due to the recession, there were many empty restaurants, so we thought, "Why not take over a space temporarily, and have a pop-up restaurant?" We called it The Hunger, and the concept was inspired by the secret dining rooms of Cuba called *paladares*. Pop-ups in general didn't exist back then; it was new and smart, and we sold out each night.

Soon after that, I started food styling and working more in food media. I loved food styling but knew I couldn't make a living from it, and I wanted to refocus my efforts on exploring how I wanted to push real food forward to the masses. In 2014, I returned to the restaurant world and opened Navy. When I think about the food I am the happiest about in my career, it is the food I created at Navy, at a time when I had a lot of freedom and great support. The people I worked with gave me so much power and confidence to do things that weren't really being done: having a beautiful little menu, writing it by hand every day, changing it up, working with local ingredients, doing great small plates, and so on. They say necessity is the mother of invention, and working only with vegetables and fish made my creativity burst forth. The food scene at that time was about little plates with the vegetable as the star, and I made a name for myself in this scene.

Unfortunately, for many reasons, we had to close the restaurant. But during this time, a little coffee shop named Café Henrie had just opened near me, and their chef hadn't worked out. The owner asked me to do a pop-up there. I agreed, thinking I would do it for the month. He wanted to get started right away. It was January, which coincided with a cleanse I was doing. I decided to base the menu off of what I was eating during this cleanse, and it was from there that my concept of healthful bowls really took off. These bowls were my modern take on a macro bowl: more flavorful, more colorful, and full of different elements that were delicious and interesting. The pop-up was a huge success from the beginning. Six months later (to think it was supposed to be a month!), my time at Café Henrie was over. Life took me to Paris, where I did a series of pop-ups. Back in New York City, I was brought in to conceptualize the restaurant De Maria, which included bringing in the team, helping design the interior, and developing the menu.

But after my time there, I was burned out on the restaurant business and its harsh, mercenary culture. I felt tired and uninspired. I started traveling a lot, cooking big dinners for big people all over the world. I was being flown to tour wine and olive oil harvests. I let myself explore new colors, textures, and meal concepts. I fed my spirit.

My style of cooking today—healthful, colorful, seasonal, and simple—is a culmination of all my experiences in the kitchen. Allowing myself this time and space helped me reinvigorate my love for cooking and inspired me to write this cookbook to share this love with you. I'm often asked how I come up with a dish, and the assumption is that I just throw things at the wall and see what sticks. But the truth is that inspiring and successful dishes follow a basic formula, and anyone with a vocabulary of sauces and finishes can be successful in the kitchen.

BRIGHT COOKING is full of vibrant and colorful plates, but it's also a love letter to smart, clever, sharp, and intuitive cooking. The dishes in this book expand upon the ways food can be experienced and shared—it will teach you how to understand the aspects of a dish so you can mix and match and combine the elements to create your own. In the years that I've been cooking, it's been so special to see the journey food has taken, and how it has become such an important part of popular culture. It's been fun to watch people get into cooking for each other and connect with themselves and their own cultural histories through food.

My hope is that BRIGHT COOKING inspires you to cook for yourself, but also for each other. Cooking is one of the most personal things you can do—I've always said nothing shows you care more than making dinner for someone. Taking the time to understand their palate, shopping for their favorites, and feeding them a dish that will delight and nourish them is the ultimate gift, a devoted act of love. The world would be a better place if we took the time to cook for each other.

So, I invite you to slow down. Plan your meal, shop for your ingredients thoughtfully, cook intuitively, plate your meal intentionally, set the table. Food is an incredible offering; savor your time with it.

GIVENCHY

WHAT
is
BRIGHT
COOKING?

I started cooking more at home during the COVID-19 pandemic, and I am sure this cookbook would've been very different if the pandemic hadn't happened while I was writing it. I realized home cooking and restaurant cooking are distinct, and I wanted to apply the tips and techniques I had learned in restaurants to cooking at home.

I want BRIGHT COOKING to demystify the practice of listening to your body and honing your instincts to cook in a healthy and intuitive way. I've divided the book into two sections: Elements and Dishes. The Elements section outfits your pantry, giving you the freedom and security to trust yourself, mix and match, and come up with your own dishes while listening to your body and what it needs that day to function at its best. The Dishes section includes hits from my career as a New York City restaurant chef, but you should approach this section aspirationally—don't let the need to make these dishes exactly as I've written them stifle your creativity.

BRIGHT COOKING is about bringing you the most important things I've learned throughout my career and taking responsibility to support sustainable foodways, shop farmers' markets, or buy organic to help support the foundation for what is our birthright: delicious, flavor-packed, nutrient-rich food. Due to concerns about climate change, I have chosen not to include any meat or poultry dishes in this book. The majority of the output of the meat and poultry industry in the United States is toxic to consume and damages our earth. Even though I do cook with meat from time to time, I'm highly conscious of where my meat comes from; otherwise, I won't buy it.

The foundation of my cooking follows four main tenets: cooking is sensorial, eating is intuitive, be responsible in your sourcing, and adventure is essential.

Cooking is sensorial.

Cooking from an intentional place is about using all your senses at once: sound, scent, taste, touch, sight, and intuition. You need to engage each of these senses to develop your cooking into a meditative practice.

SOUND Food talks in its sizzle, pop, gurgle, and boil. Usually, when I cook big meals, I don't play music. Why? Because I want to hear if something is sizzling too hard or if the gurgle is too light because that tells me the heat is too high or too low. When toasting sesame seeds, you need to listen closely for that one-two pop, which means they're starting to toast. Once they're all popping and going off, you know it's ready. Food talks to you, and you need to listen.

SCENT Aroma is a memory connector, and when we cook without a cookbook, aroma demonstrates where you are in the process. After you've been cooking for a long time, you can smell if something is missing, because you've learned what it's supposed to smell like when it's finished. This is one of those chef's instincts that develops with time. If you're in tune with smelling, you can catch things before they burn. Engaging with scent helps you realize when the foods are moving forward and evolving. You are connecting with it on a different level.

TASTE You always want to be tasting your meal from the very beginning to the end, not only because you want your end product to be great, but also because it helps you connect to its journey. You are relating to your food. Flavors shift: The dish might need more salt, or it might need more acid, and you are facilitating. Many flavors are based on a balance of salt, acid, and heat, among many others. All of them should align, and one shouldn't overpower the other unless it is intentional. That's what makes a balanced flavor.

TOUCH This is a sense we are not usually very connected to when cooking, but it's a mighty one. You want to connect with food to understand its process and temperature. The more a fish cooks, the more changes to its density will occur, and that's why you touch the fish each minute to understand how it's coming along. When making yogurt, I put my finger in the milk to sense the temperature. We also use our sense of touch as an indicator of ripeness or freshness at the market when shopping for vegetables and fruit or understanding the doneness when cooking proteins. There is a delicacy that you need to fine-tune when you touch food. When you are at the market, every vegetable and fruit has a different way of telling you when it is ready or past its peak: The harder a mango is, the less ripe it is; if a tomato or an avocado feels mushy, that means it's overripe.

SIGHT The most noticeable part of the cooking process is how the ingredients visually shift and change. When I want to make something, I visualize what it will look like by the end. The act of visualization helps in the act of being intentional when you cook, and sight is a great way to ensure that. It's important not only in the process of cooking but also when it comes to plating and offering the dish to someone else. During my fine dining days, I worked with a specific chef who approached color in his work in a beautiful way. That very much inspired me, and I refer to it still when I'm on set as a food stylist, or when I'm developing a story for a magazine, or when I'm a chef in a restaurant. Even though I don't do fine dining, it still defines so much of how I see a plate. They say you eat with your eyes. What does that mean? It is the beginning of your experience. What happens when you get a beautiful, cared-for dish? It lures you in and dictates a lot of your eating experience. You know when you see really tasty food; you just know. Now it becomes all about re-creating what tasty food looks like to you.

INTUITION It's the sixth sense. Once you master all the other senses, this one develops naturally. After cooking for many years, I began to teach classes and young chefs who worked for me. I realized that I was making certain dishes without really understanding why I was doing them that way. I had done it so often that I wasn't thinking about it. It was instinctual. In teaching, I had to develop a more profound sense of understanding because I had to explain it to someone else. The more you cook, the more you operate from a special place of instinctual flow. It's a beautiful thing because you understand something so well, and you are so immersed in it that you are not thinking about it. You know what your palate wants. And instinctively, you are able to fine-tune it to accommodate that flavor that your palate is looking for.

Eating is intuitive.

One of my key beliefs is that your body will always tell you what it needs to feel nourished, so it's important to begin developing your intuition before you even step into the kitchen. After all, food fosters emotional connection with others, so why shouldn't it be a way to connect with yourself?

For me, the cooking journey starts with sourcing great product. Every Wednesday, I go to my local farmers' market and practice listening to my body. I take in the produce and notice what is at the peak stage of ripeness. Suddenly, I am overwhelmed with a need to buy the fragrant, glistening strawberries. I see this as my body telling me it needs antioxidants and vitamin C. I keep browsing, taking in the sights of the different vendors and their wares, the brightly colored fruits, the earthy vegetables; I stop in front of a bunch of carrots and connect with them. My body is telling me that I need some beta-carotene. I keep the questions coming: Is my body craving something fresh, crunchy? Do I want something nourishing, like a mineral-rich mushroom broth, or do I want the comfort of mashed potatoes? The more I ask my body what it needs, the easier it is for me to create nourishing meals because I am actively developing this conversation.

When you realize that cooking and meditation are connected, suddenly everything you do is imbued with purpose and intention. You connect with yourself to understand why you want the things you want: Is it a craving because you want an emotional experience, or is it what your body needs? Ultimately, when you're done eating, you want to feel emotionally and physically nourished. What we are going for is the experience. Food should look pleasing, its flavors should have dimension and depth, but most importantly, food should make you feel good after you eat it.

This is one of the main reasons that I make it my mission to eat locally, and I hope that my lifestyle, which is reflected throughout this cookbook, provides a sense of understanding and motivates you to eat locally as well. The reason it is vital to do so is because our bodies are connected to the seasons. We naturally acclimate to them. It's a big principle of macrobiotic cuisine to always eat food that grows in the area you are in because your body is going to digest it with ease and readily absorb more nutrients. Also, when food travels from other climates, it loses its nutrients and its life force.

I firmly believe that anyone can develop a beautiful dish that is based on seasonality, on hunger and cravings. But to me, one of the most important things to have in the kitchen, above good ingredients, is your desire to create. Sometimes when you follow a recipe, you become so involved and absorbed in the process—Did I miss a step? Was that the right moment to add this ingredient?—that you stop cooking and instead engage in a more mechanical act. Without wanting to, you zap all the creativity out of cooking.

I believe in pantry prep instead of meal prep. I want you to have an outfitted pantry that lets you develop dishes from what you already have available, so you can make creative, impulsive, intuitive dishes as the spirit moves you, rather than picking from premade food stored in the fridge. This cookbook will help you create wonderful sauces, nut mixes, powders, and more so that you

have them ready and in hand to spice up any fresh ingredients you bring home. Say you went to the farmers' market and cucumbers were inexpensive because they were in peak season. So you buy a bunch. From here, you can pickle them with Pickled Mustard Seed (page 78) or Cucumber and Dulse Pickle (page 76). Or, toss them with lemon and salt, and serve them with roasted nuts and Herby Sorrel Yogurt sauce (page 37). Maybe you're not in the mood to put together an involved meal. Ah! You picked some vegetables at the market, so can you steam them, add some Toasted Cacao Nib, Buckwheat, and Sesame Mix (page 108) and a beautiful sesame oil for a thrown-together treat.

Bright Cooking is about motivating you to have a beautiful pantry of flourishes and inspiring you to create based on what you have in your kitchen and what you hunger for, while also developing an ongoing communication with your body and what your body is communicating it needs. By the end of this book, I want you to cook by instinct instead of recipes, to become fully immersed in the process of how an ingredient transforms itself from raw to cooked.

Be responsible in your sourcing.

If there is one thing you take away from this cookbook, I want it to be the following: Make it your mission to shop locally and seasonally.

As I mentioned earlier, our bodies are connected to the seasons. Being mindful of the varieties of fruits and vegetables carried through by our ancestors is part of my philosophy as a chef. Eating a zucchini picked hours before it reaches your plate is a delicious practice full of vital energy. When all the systems are aligned—like optimum soil health mixed with an exceptional growing season and low pollution—the fruits of that labor are ripe, juicy, flavorful, nutritious, and full of vitamins and minerals. Not to mention, it's been scientifically proven that the more flavorful the fruit, the more nutrients it possesses.

While it feels convenient to have access to strawberries all year round, the practice of buying something out of season and out of our hemisphere has a negative effect on our bodies and planet. Our food systems are based on what I like to call factory-farmed foods. When you go to the supermarket and notice the labels, you'll see how most of the produce isn't grown locally. Every vegetable and fruit from the supermarket is bred and crossbred so the seed can grow the same everywhere and withstand different environments. We are forced to consume these nutrient-deficient products by the industrial agricultural complex, which is why it is such a struggle to keep our bodies healthy when we don't eat right.

What makes this even worse is that it takes a significant toll on our environment to transport food from one place to another. When you buy a product from another country or region, the traveling process slowly eats away at the product's vital force. The taste changes, it becomes bland, and bland fruits and vegetables are nutrient-depleted.

I know it takes time and effort to find and go to these markets, but it is our responsibility to try and force ourselves out of our supermarket comfort zones. Countries like Italy and Spain never lost the connection to their roots, while the United States is barely in the process of rebuilding the foundation of a sound system. Our local farmers deserve to be recognized and valued in our economy, and we must do everything we can to support them. They grow delicious food, and eating it is our birthright, just like it is our birthright to have healthy bodies thanks to the food we put in them. Shopping at the farmers' market means you're maximizing on nutrients and gaining more flavor, all while revitalizing the farming culture.

Trust me. Your patience will be rewarded with an explosion of flavor when something you love is in season for you. You will be personally connected to the movement of the seasons and traveling through its edible offerings. The ultimate luxury is being able to eat delicious food that makes you happy. If we can ensure that people from all walks of life eat fruits and vegetables grown on their land, we will be in a better place, and our land will thank us with its bounty.

Adventure is essential.

I gain many lessons about technique and ingredients when traveling that make their way into my cooking. One of my favorite dishes is still fish poached in seawater from a trip I took to the Yucatán Peninsula nearly eighteen years ago. How did I learn the technique? I asked the restaurant how they did it. They told me they take the seawater and let it sit for a few days, so the sediment sinks down to the bottom. They then carefully scoop the water from the top, boil it, then use it as a cooking broth.

The adventure of finding ingredients or techniques is a big part of *Bright Cooking*. When you travel and taste something you love, don't be afraid to ask questions: How is it prepared? What is in it? All of this is adventure-seeking, which I believe is essential to cooking and learning.

The first thing I do when traveling is find the local farmers' market, one of the biggest areas of culture within a city. I buy fruit or snacks for my trip. Even if I don't need to buy anything, I go. Every farmers' market throughout the world helps you understand its culture. It shows you how people eat, convene, and get along, and it introduces you to ingredients you might've never seen before.

Research the area's food traditions when planning a trip, just as you would take time to find a hotel with a good view or a restaurant with great reviews. Find a specific tradition you are interested in learning about, and seek out food tours or even cooking classes taught by locals

in their homes. Make travel plans to a specific place because you've heard of its food scene or trends. My daughter and I always travel because we (and by we, I mean I) want to know more about a specific trend, tradition, or style of food the area is known for.

However, you shouldn't limit this type of exploration to only when you are traveling abroad. One time we traveled to Ithaca, New York, a four-hour trip from home, just to eat at Moosewood Café, because *The Moosewood Cookbook* was the first cookbook I connected to growing up.

Instead of escaping your hometown for the beach, visit that farm you always shop from at the farmers' market. Connecting with the people who work at the farm and learning about what goes into their produce helps develop a deeper sensibility of your food and an almost spiritual relationship to it. Learn about how they treat the soil and what goes into growing. Maybe you will even discover a new favorite vegetable or way of preparing it that you've never tried before. You could even offer to help out a little.

Ultimately, I want you to follow your food curiosity when traveling, so you make seeking out restaurants and foodways a permanent part of your travel experience. This is a surefire way to open yourself to food, culture, and even history. Most of all, it helps deepen your connection to the world. Always try to fit in some food adventure, no matter what you do or where you go.

On Ingredients

At the end of the day, I'm all about steering people toward the most natural, least processed ingredients in their cooking. I stick to ingredients that are local when I can. For example, in New York we use maple syrup as a sweetener, but if you live in Arizona or southern California, you might use agave instead. In Florida, perhaps good cane sugar is available to you.

Honey is everywhere, and it's best if you can find super-local honey (it's good for allergies). If you're using super-floral honey but cooking it, the subtle notes likely won't come through, so find ways to let it really shine, like drizzling it on toast or atop yogurt. We're so accustomed to using white sugar, but it's so bad for so many people. Why not use sugars with greater depths of flavor and other benefits to our bodies? These regional ingredients will bring flavor, color, and uniqueness to your cooking.

We can't just lie down and accept bland factory-farmed foods.

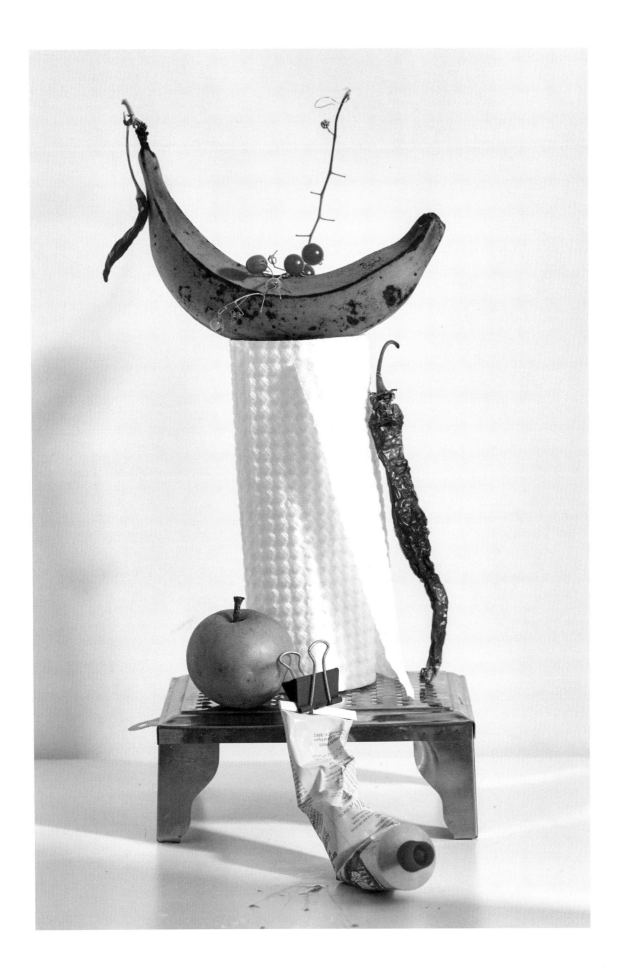

ELEMENTS

As a professional chef, your "mise en place" is an organized workstation with all the essential elements that go into a dish. Having everything in its place and ready to go before you begin to cook will ensure you have a successful service when it's time to perform. This section is about building a strong, foundational collection of elements in your pantry so you can be ready to go whenever the inspiration strikes.

I know it's strange to write this in a cookbook, but I don't like relying on recipes; I trust my body to tell me what it needs, and my meticulously stocked pantry serves as my arsenal to achieve that. A well-stocked pantry is like a culinary toolbox, full of the tools you need to assemble a dish developed by your intuition, mood, and appetite. I want you to learn to listen to your body so you can understand what it wants, and have the confidence to use the elements in your pantry as you follow the muse. Recipes are a nice start, but ultimately, cooking intuitively means considering accessibility, seasonality, locality, and cravings.

At their core, all dishes can be broken down in the following way: the star item, a sauce, and a flourish. Consider flourishes as the supporting cast of your plate: a delicious sprinkling of a salty, spicy, or crunchy element. Let's say you get home after a long day and say, "Oh gosh, I don't feel like a cooking project, so I'm just going to steam a fish and some turnips." What's the star of the dish? The fish and turnips. What about the sauce? It can be a beautiful sesame oil or the Green Tahini (page 54) you've made ahead. What's the flourish? Sesame, Cranberry Seed, and Safflower Gomasio (page 106) and Crispy Honey Chili Oil (page 118) or a Salsa Verde (page 64) with spicy pepitas. One time I made a dish that everyone loved and kept asking me what was in it. It was just a basic meat and potatoes dish topped with a mix of two different mother sauces: tahini dressing and a hollandaise. They were unexpected yet incredibly delicious when paired with a tried-and-true base.

This process mirrors my formulaic approach to creating dishes in a restaurant. You start with an arsenal of accoutrements, finishes, and flourishes at your disposal, and then you carefully combine them into a lovely, vibrant meal. All the foundational elements in this section can play with each other in different ways. After you work your way through this section, my hope is that you'll only be a smear of this, a few sprinkles of that, and a pinch of flourish away from confidence and creative freedom in the kitchen.

MODERN MOTHER SAUCES

More often than not, dishes benefit from extra sauce and dressing, and I like my dishes to be juicy and saucy. Whether your sauce is tangy, spicy, or salty, it is the best and most effective way to pack the most flavor into a dish.

When I went to culinary school, I was taught classical French cuisine, an haute cuisine style based on the sixteenth- to eighteenth-century grand kitchens, that utilizes five mother sauces as the basis for all dishes:

BÉCHAMEL: milk with a flour-thickened base

ESPAGNOLE: a dark stock with tomato concentrate and a flour-thickened base

HOLLANDAISE: a warm emulsion of clarified butter and egg yolk

TOMATO: a simple tomato sauce

VELOUTÉ: a light stock with a flour-thickened base

These sauces were so crucial that during that time, the position of saucier was the third most important person in the kitchen after the chef and the sous chef. However, times have changed; most people don't eat like that anymore. We have less time to dedicate to composing indulgent sauces like the demiglace, which takes four days to make. Nowadays, we are more conscious about what we eat as well. That doesn't mean sauces have lost their importance. The principle still applies: They are a vital part of a composed dish and have a nutritional purpose.

What I like to call "modern mother sauces" are lighter and easier to make and do not require a lot of technique, making the art of cooking more accessible than it once was. In my experience, I've found that the following sauces are the most commonly used in modern cookery and they are a reflection of our palate today:

YOGURTS AND CULTURED CREAMS: tangy, bright, and rich with protein

VINAIGRETTES, CITRONETTES, AND MOJOS: light and acidic

SEED AND NUT SAUCES: rich and dense

EGG-BASED SAUCES: rich, silky, and umami-filled

HERB SAUCES AND PESTOS: big, verdant, and energizing

BUTTER SAUCES: traditional but versatile

As in previous times, sauces should still be one of the most important elements of your dish—aside from the star ingredient, the sauce is what will infuse your dish with juicy flavor. And sauces are so versatile. For instance, I'll make a yogurt sauce in the beginning of the week for a particular dish, then whatever I have left over, I dollop on flatbread or a grain bowl, mix into a dressing, or use as a dip for a crunchy veg. I like to stock my fridge with one or two of these sauces every week. Having these sauces as an ever-present element in your arsenal creates an ease in the kitchen. It's an element you can rely upon when you're hungry and want something quick and nourishing.

YOGURTS AND CULTURED CREAMS

Yogurt sauces come together quickly and easily while still being balanced and delicious. Even something as simple as combining yogurt and sea salt can make a great little dipping sauce. Yogurt-based sauces are lush and bright, which complement a range of flavors, from subtle to fatty to spicy hot. When homemade, yogurt has a slight sweetness that plays well with its tang to create a perfect balance of flavors. In the recipes that follow, you can use cultured cream or sour cream instead of yogurt to make a more decadent sauce for a special occasion. The best vegan yogurts I've come across are those that cook the starches of nuts and oats to thicken, then culture it for tanginess and probiotic health factors. My Vegan Yogurt Master Recipe (page 35) has you heating the cashew cream until it thickens, then adding the yogurt starter to let it culture for a creamy finish.

Whole-Milk Yogurt Master Recipe

MAKES 1 QUART [960 ML]

4 cups [240 ml] whole milk

¼ cup [60 g] plain full-fat yogurt

In a medium saucepan over low heat, warm the milk to 180°F [82°C]. Remove from the heat and let cool by stirring occasionally until it reaches 108°F [42°C]. Whisk in the yogurt until completely combined with the milk. Transfer to a lidded clean glass or plastic container and keep in the oven with just the oven light or pilot on or in a warm place in your kitchen until firm, 1 to 2 days. For a thicker consistency, strain the yogurt for an additional 8 hours in a strainer fitted with cheesecloth. For an even richer and almost cream cheese–like consistency, referred to as labneh, strain for an additional day. Store in a lidded container in the refrigerator and use within 2 weeks.

Vegan Yogurt Master Recipe

MAKES 3 CUPS [680 G]

1 cup [100 g] rolled oats

4 cups [960 ml] filtered or spring water

1 cup [125 g] whole raw cashews

½ tsp salt

1 Tbsp vegan yogurt culture or ¼ cup [60 g] vegan yogurt from a previous batch

¼ cup [60 ml] vinegar or lemon juice

Add the oats and filtered water to a blender. Blend for 30 seconds. Line a strainer with cheesecloth and drain. Rinse the blender and transfer the strained mixture back in. Add the whole cashews and salt and blend until smooth, about 1 minute. Transfer the mixture to a medium saucepot and whisk constantly over medium heat until its consistency is a bit thicker than gravy. Remove from the heat and cool to 110°F [43°C], using an ice bath or letting it cool naturally. Sprinkle in the vegan yogurt culture and vinegar and keep in a warm environment, either a yogurt maker or the oven with the light on, for 8 hours. The idea is to keep it at 110°F [43°C].

Store in a lidded container in the refrigerator for 1 week. Note that after 3 days it becomes more tart in flavor.

Tahini Yogurt

MAKES 1 CUP [240 G]

1 tsp tahini

1 cup [240 g] yogurt, preferably Whole-Milk Yogurt Master Recipe (page 35)

Pinch salt

In a small bowl, combine the tahini with a couple of spoonfuls of the yogurt. Whisk until well combined, then slowly add the remaining yogurt and salt. Whisk again to combine fully. (This process ensures no tahini lumps.) Store in a lidded container in the refrigerator for 10 days.

Uses
I love this with fresh or preserved fruit with a sprinkle of sesame seeds or Fruit Powder (page 115). For savory applications, finish with a drizzle of spiced or chili oil and crunchy sea salt for use as a dip or dressing for crunchy salad.

Dish
Fruit Bowl (page 126)

Beet-Dill Yogurt

MAKES 1½ CUPS [360 G]

½ cup [120 g] cooked, peeled, and coarsely chopped beets

¼ jalapeño, seeded and finely chopped

1 garlic clove, minced or finely grated

¼ tsp sea salt

¼ cup [15 g] fresh dill (roughly half a bunch), thick stems removed, roughly chopped

1 cup [240 g] yogurt, preferably Whole-Milk Yogurt Master Recipe (page 35)

1 tsp vinegar

In a food processor, combine the beets, jalapeño, garlic, and salt and process until well minced. Add the dill and pulse three or four times, enough to coarsely chop, but do not overdo it. You should still see pieces of every ingredient. Add the yogurt and vinegar, pulsing a couple times to incorporate. Store in a lidded container in the refrigerator for 10 days.

Uses
This makes a zippy dip for crudités and fritters. It goes great with crispy smashed sweet potatoes, topped with walnuts and olives. Make it a meal by serving it with a salad, piece of cheese, hard-boiled egg, or fish and flatbread to accompany.

Dish
Crudo (page 236)

Curry Leaf Yogurt

MAKES 1 CUP [240 G]

1 Tbsp neutral oil, such as sunflower, grapeseed, safflower, or rice bran

2 sprigs fresh curry leaves (approximately 15 leaves)

1 cup [240 g] strained yogurt (see Note), preferably Whole-Milk Yogurt Master Recipe (page 35)

1 Tbsp vinegar or fresh lemon juice

Drizzle of natural liquid sweetener, such as maple syrup, honey, agave, or date syrup

Couple grates of citrus zest (optional)

Pinch salt

Pinch chili powder

In a small pan over medium heat, warm the oil. Very carefully add the fresh curry leaves to the oil. They will pop, so stand back when doing so. Pull them out 30 seconds after the first pop is heard—they should be translucent. Let drain on paper towels until cool.

In a medium bowl, mix together the yogurt, vinegar, sweetener, zest (if using), salt, and chili powder. Crumble the curry leaves with your fingers into the yogurt and discard the stems. Let the yogurt sit in the refrigerator for 2 hours so that the curry flavor and aroma can infuse. Store in a lidded container in the refrigerator for 10 days.

NOTE: To strain yogurt, place a fine-mesh sieve over a bowl and line with cheesecloth or a clean tea towel. Add the yogurt and allow it to sit and strain for 30 minutes, until thickened. The longer it sits, the thicker it will be. Discard the whey (or find another use for it).

Uses
Serve this with a summer tomato and white onion salad, or dollop it on dal, spicy curries, and chili.

Dish
Stuffed Crispy Grape Leaves with Curry Leaf Yogurt and Pine Nuts (page 155)

Herby Sorrel Yogurt

MAKES 1 CUP [240 G]

1 cup [40 g] coarsely chopped sorrel leaf (or other soft herb, see Note)

¼ cup [10 g] mint leaves, loosely packed

1 Tbsp capers

¼ cup [60 ml] neutral oil

½ cup [120 g] cultured cream (see Note, below) or strained yogurt (see Note, left)

2 pinches sea salt

In a food processor or blender, add the sorrel, mint, capers, and oil and process until smooth, approximately 30 seconds. If blending, start slowly and work up in speed. Transfer to a bowl and fold in the cultured cream and salt. Store in a lidded container in the refrigerator for 10 days.

NOTE: Any soft herb will work here, though I particularly love the tangy and wild greenness of sorrel. I prefer using cultured cream with this sauce when pairing it with fish.

Uses
This is an excellent sauce for any grain bowl. It's especially nice when mixed with rice and topped with steamed sweet plantains, roasted peeled sweet potato, or an egg.

Dish
Fish en Croûte (page 252)

Fennel Pollen Yogurt

MAKES 1 CUP [240 G]

1 cup [240 g] strained yogurt (see Note on page 37), preferably Whole-Milk Yogurt Master Recipe (page 35)

½ tsp sea salt

Small drizzle of honey

1 tsp fennel pollen or 2 tsp sumac (see Note)

In a medium bowl, mix together all the ingredients until well combined and store in the refrigerator for 4 hours. This yogurt is best if you make it a few hours in advance so that the flavors and aromas have time to infuse the yogurt. Store in a lidded container in the refrigerator for 10 days.

NOTE: If you don't have, or enjoy, fennel pollen, sumac is a nice substitute (some varieties of sumac even turn the yogurt a lovely purple hue).

Uses
This is best with dishes that are fried or have some char to them. I love it on herby room-temperature frittatas, Spanish tortillas, or quesadillas with avocado and hot sauce. Try mixing in sliced cucumber, celery, or onion and an acid such as fresh lemon juice to make a tzatziki-inspired dip.

Dishes
Charred Winter Squash with Sumac Yogurt and Pistachio (page 218)

Dragon Bowl (page 224)

Sprouted Rye Berry Yogurt

MAKES 1½ CUPS [360 G]

½ cup [80 g] sprouted rye or other grain (see Note)

1 cup [240 g] Greek yogurt

2 pinches sea salt

Sprinkle of chili powder or black pepper

Cook the grains as you would pasta: Bring a large pot of water to a boil and add salt until it tastes like the ocean. Add the grains and simmer over low heat for 10 minutes. When tender, strain and let cool completely. When the grains are ready, transfer them to a medium bowl, add the yogurt, and stir to combine. Season with the salt and chili powder. Store in a lidded container in the refrigerator for 10 days.

NOTE: Although rye berries are my favorite grain for this yogurt, you can swap in wheat, farro, or barley. Tougher-skinned grains like these really do benefit from sprouting before you use them, as it improves the texture, increases nutrition, and makes them easier to digest.

Uses
For a chic, clean-out-the-refrigerator grain bowl, mix with chopped leftover vegetables, lots of fresh herbs and greens, and some oil and vinegar to taste.

Dish
Olive Oil–Poached Swordfish with Cucumber and Sprouted Rye Berry Yogurt (page 249)

Green Goddess Yogurt

MAKES 1½ CUPS [360 G]

¼ cup [60 ml] avocado oil or other neutral oil, such as sunflower, grapeseed, safflower, or rice bran

3 Tbsp fresh lemon juice or cider vinegar

2 dashes liquid aminos or fish sauce, 1 anchovy, or 1 Tbsp preserved lemon purée (optional)

2 cups [24 g] mixed soft herbs (basil, chervil, chives, cilantro, dill, mint, parsley, tarragon, or a combination)

1 avocado, peeled and pitted

¼ cup [60 g] yogurt, preferably Whole-Milk Yogurt Master Recipe (page 35)

In a food processor or blender, add the oil, lemon juice, and liquid aminos, then top with the herbs and avocado. This layering makes it easier to blend all the ingredients together. Blend until smooth without letting the mixture get too warm, adding water if the herbs are having a hard time breaking down. Add the yogurt and pulse to mix. Store in a lidded container in the refrigerator for 10 days.

Uses

This is a perfect summer dressing for a market chopped salad loaded with feta and good olive oil. In the cold months, dollop it on a baked sweet potato, especially the dense Japanese variety.

Dish

Hippie Sandwich (page 153)

CELERY
VINEGAR

DRIED
FRUIT
SPICE
4/2

VINAI-GRETTES, CITRON-ETTES, AND MOJOS

Salads are one of the easiest dishes to create, and they shine when complemented with light sauces with a punch of acidity. What differentiates each of these sauces is where the acidity originates: Vinaigrettes, as the name states, are made with vinegar; citronettes are made from citrus juice (such as lemons, limes, and oranges); and mojos can use either, but are set apart by their super garlicky flavor that's best used to marinate or complement richer or denser foods. When composing a perfect salad, I love to use the principle "If it grows together, it goes together." So, set yourself free at the farmers' market, and drizzle any seasonal finds that call to you with one of these dressings, a sprinkle of fresh herbs, and a flourish or two.

À la Minute Vinaigrette

I make most of my leafy salads at home à la min-ute, which is to say that I don't use a premade vinaigrette. The ratio to keep in mind when dressing is one part acid to three or four parts oil. I start by laying the chilled lettuces and herbs on a chilled platter or shallow bowl (I wish I was a wooden bowl salad person, but up to this point I am not). If using vinegar, I place my thumb over the bottle opening and adjust the pressure to allow for the vinegar to rain over the lettuces gently. When using lemon, I squeeze it with my hand, allowing it to shower over all the lettuces, while holding my other hand under-neath to catch the seeds. The lettuces can sit like this for a quite some time—as they sit, they soak up the acid. Next, drizzle on the oil. Now the seasoning has something to stick to. Sprinkle on salt, black pepper or chili powder, and maybe some sesame seeds from high up so they cover more area as they land. Toss right before you serve it. Before plating, pick up a leaf to taste and confirm the flavors are right, and adjust if needed.

Black Sesame–Chili Vinaigrette

MAKES 1½ CUPS [360 ML]

½ cup [70 g] toasted black sesame seeds

1 tsp salt

¾ cup [180 ml] grapeseed oil

¼ cup [60 ml] sesame oil

¼ cup [60 ml] rice vinegar

¼ tsp chili powder or urfa pepper flakes

In a mortar, combine the sesame seeds and salt and pound with the pestle until most of the sesame seeds have been coarsely ground (every seed should be nicked). Transfer to a small bowl and stir in the oils, vinegar, and chili powder. Use immediately or store at room temperature for 2 weeks or in the refrigerator for 3 months.

Uses

This vinaigrette is perfect on a simple salad of chilled leaf lettuces, raw crunchy salads, or crudi-tés. It's also great drizzled over grain bowls such as the Dragon Bowl (page 224).

Dish

Dragon Bowl (page 224)

Citronette

MAKES ½ CUP [120 ML]

¼ cup [60 ml] fresh lemon juice

1½ Tbsp sweetener, such as maple syrup, honey, or agave

¼ cup [60 ml] neutral oil, such as sunflower, grapeseed, safflower, or rice bran

In a medium bowl, whisk together the lemon juice and sweetener until the sugars have dissolved into the lemon juice. The mixture should taste like sweet lemonade. Gradually whisk in the oil; when it thickens and has the density of dressing, stop adding the oil. When making it for the first time, it's helpful to follow the measurements above, but try to take note of the key sensorial markers within the process. It's a great way to develop your instincts, making it easier to scale to how much is needed or how much of each ingredient you have on hand. Use immediately or store at room temperature for 1 week or in the refrigerator for 2 months.

Uses

A salad dressing at any time of the year: summer salads with melon, onion, and spicy almonds; autumn salads with endives, roasted root vegetables, and roasted hazelnuts (see page 105); winter salads of beets and oranges with pickled onion and yogurt or crumbled feta; and spring salads with peppery arugula, dates, and roasted walnuts (see page 105).

Dishes

Rhubarb, Napa Cabbage, and Watermelon Radish Salad in Big Flavor Dressing (page 180)

Endive and Parsnip Salad with Pistachio, Blue Cheese, and Citronette (page 185)

Collard Green and Peach Summer Salad (page 193)

Cucumber, Plum, and Ricotta with Citronette (page 190)

Shaved Mushroom, Dandelion, and Petal Salad (page 197)

Honey-Miso Dressing

MAKES 1 CUP [340 ML]

⅓ cup [80 ml] rice wine vinegar

2 Tbsp light miso

1 Tbsp honey

½ cup [120 ml] grapeseed oil

In a medium bowl, add the vinegar and miso and whisk to break down the miso until you achieve a smooth consistency. Whisk in the honey until dissolved. Gradually whisk in the oil. Store in a lidded container in the refrigerator for 1 month.

Uses

This dressing loves hearty raw greens such as kale and chicories and works divinely with raw napa cabbage mixed with other crunchy vegetables and sprinkled with roasted peanuts or sesame seed mix (see page 105).

Dish

Chicories and Seaweeds (page 187)

Big Flavor Dressing

MAKES ¼ CUP [60 ML]

¼ cup [60 ml] fresh lime juice

1 Tbsp fish sauce

1 Tbsp maple syrup

Coarse black pepper, chili flakes, or sliced fresh chile

In a small bowl, add the lime juice, fish sauce, maple syrup, and pepper and mix well. Use immediately or store at room temperature for 1 week or in the refrigerator for 2 months.

Uses
This dressing has no oil, so it really penetrates dishes with flavor and imparts bold energy. It's perfect for salads comprised of vegetables that need more flavor than others, such as cucumber, jicama, and celery, and topped with chile flakes and toasted sesame seeds or roasted peanuts (see page 105).

Dishes
Watermelon Salad with Turmeric-Ginger Relish (page 189)

Smoked Fish Salad with Daikon, Asian Pear, and Poppy Seeds (page 201)

Steamed sweet plantains (see page 212) with Crispy Honey Chili Oil (page 118)

Rhubarb, Napa Cabbage, and Watermelon Radish Salad with Big Flavor Dressing (page 180)

Almond Milk Vinaigrette

MAKES 1½ CUPS [360 ML]

¼ cup [60 ml] neutral oil, such as sunflower, grapeseed, safflower, or rice bran

3 Tbsp full-fat Greek yogurt, crème fraîche, or sour cream

1 Tbsp vinegar

½ tsp maple syrup, honey, or agave

½ tsp fish sauce

1 cup [240 ml] high-quality almond milk, preferably homemade

In a medium bowl, add the oil, yogurt, vinegar, syrup, and fish sauce and whisk to combine. Add the almond milk and whisk to combine. Use immediately or store in the refrigerator for 1 week.

Uses
This delicate dressing is best paired with subtle ingredients, such as a salad of peas with Baby Gem leaves and mint or steamed onions with almonds and a drizzle of olive oil, spiced oil, or chili oil.

Dish
Cucumber and Apricot Salad with Almond Milk Vinaigrette (page 192)

Pecan-Coconut Dressing

MAKES 1 CUP [240 ML]

½ cup [70 g] roasted pecans or other nuts (see page 105)

½ cup [120 ml] coconut cream

2 Tbsp fresh lemon juice or vinegar

Pinch salt

Pinch chili powder

½ tsp toasted cumin seeds

½ tsp toasted mustard seeds

1 tsp Asian ground mustard (such as S&B)

In a food processor or blender, add the pecans, coconut cream, and lemon juice. Pulse four times, until the nuts have broken down slightly. Stir in the salt, chili powder, cumin seeds, mustard seeds, and ground mustard. This keeps for 3 days in the refrigerator.

Uses
Add to shredded cabbage with sliced white onion and serve as an accompaniment for spicy curries or to top a grain bowl.

Dish
Napa Cabbage, Coconut, and Pecan Salad with Pecan-Coconut Dressing (page 183)

Leche de Tigre

MAKES 1 CUP [240 ML]

½ cup [120 ml] coconut milk

½ cup [120 ml] fresh lime juice

¼ tsp salt

¼ tsp chili powder

In a small bowl, combine the coconut milk, lime juice, salt, and chili powder and mix well. This keeps for 3 days in the refrigerator.

Uses
This is traditionally used as a ceviche marinade in Mexico and Central America mixed with fish, hominy, and sweet potato. I suggest you add lots of chopped cilantro and use it as a dip for fried snacks.

Dish
Tiger Bowl (page 227)

Dal Fritters with Leche de Tigre (page 165)

Toast (page 169)

Ginger-Garlic Mojo

MAKES ¾ CUP [180 ML]

3 Tbsp minced or grated ginger

3 Tbsp minced or grated garlic

½ cup [120 ml] fresh lemon juice

Pinch salt

4 turns freshly cracked pepper

Add the ginger and garlic to a small bowl and cover with the lemon juice. Let it sit for 15 minutes to cure. Add the salt and pepper to finish. Use immediately or store at room temperature for 1 week or in the refrigerator for 2 months.

Uses

This sauce is most popular for marinating meats; serving with steamed whole-root vegetables, such as parsnips, carrots, yucca, and rutabagas; and as a dip for fritters of all kinds—the tartness cuts right through the richness of fried foods.

Dishes

Corn and Chickpea Fritters with Ginger-Garlic Mojo (page 152)

Salt-Baked Vegetables with Cacao Seed Mix (page 209)

SEED AND NUT SAUCES

Seed and nut sauces are mainstays in my kitchen because of their versatile nature: They provide rich umami flavor, they enrich dishes with protein, and they are fantastic for thickening saucy dishes such as curries and stews. It doesn't take much to make these beautiful sauces, and using premade nut butters as your base is a speedy way to add depth in a pinch. Add citrus, fresh herbs, cooked vegetables, or spices to zhuzh it up. I usually grate some garlic, add some lemon to it to cure for a bit, then mix in tahini or nut paste, adding small amounts of water at a time to thin it out for a lovely sauce or a wonderful dressing for a simple salad of romaine or kale. Puréed cooked beets or carrots buzzed with sunflower butter or peanut butter and finished with some citrus and/or vinegar is another quick standard. Next time you make a stewy dish, try adding a little seed or nut paste and see how nicely the nut butter gives it body.

Nutty Seedy Sauce Master Recipe

MAKES 1 CUP [240 G]

¼ cup [60 g] nut or seed butter

3 Tbsp lemon juice or vinegar

1 Tbsp (or more) flavor element, such as cured garlic or shallot (see Note), mustard, miso, chopped kimchi, or ¼ cup [5 g] chopped herbs

¼ tsp salt

In a medium bowl or small food processor, add the nut butter and lemon juice. Whisk or blend until smooth.

Add your flavor element of choice and whisk or blend again until smooth. At this point, the mixture may look broken or too thick. If so, gradually add ¼ cup [60 ml] or more water slowly while whisking or blending until the mixture reaches the consistency of a Caesar dressing. Add the salt and stir to combine. Store in a lidded container in the refrigerator for 1 week.

NOTE: Curing raw garlic or shallot removes some of its sharpness, making it more palatable. To make, cover 1 Tbsp minced garlic or shallot with 1 Tbsp lemon juice or vinegar. Let sit for 10 minutes before using.

Beet–Sunflower Seed Sauce

MAKES ABOUT 1 CUP [240 G]

1 medium beet, cooked, peeled, and chopped

¼ cup [35 g] sunflower seeds

¼ cup [60 ml] filtered water, plus more as needed

3 Tbsp neutral oil, such as sunflower, grapeseed, safflower, or rice bran

2 Tbsp vinegar

2 tsp miso

1 tsp honey

Pinch salt

Pinch chili powder

In a blender, add all the ingredients and process until smooth. If the blender is having a hard time processing, add a spoonful of water at a time until the sauce reaches the desired consistency. Store in a lidded container in the refrigerator for 1 week.

Uses
Dip bread, vegetables, or tart fruit into the sauce and then into a savory seed mix for a twist on crudités with a ton of texture.

Dish
Tiger Bowl (page 226)

Green Tahini

MAKES 1¼ CUPS [300 G]

¼ cup [60 ml] neutral oil, such as sunflower, grapeseed, safflower, or rice bran

2 Tbsp vinegar

2 Tbsp filtered water, plus more as needed

1 Tbsp preserved lemon purée or 2 Tbsp fresh lemon juice or vinegar

½ tsp salt

1 cup [20 g] soft herbs, such as parsley, chervil, chives, or sorrel; or rich soft greens, such as spinach or arugula

½ cup [110 g] tahini

In a blender, add the oil, vinegar, water, preserved lemon, and salt and process until smooth. Add the herbs and tahini and process until smooth. While the blender is still running, add more water 1 Tbsp at a time until the sauce reaches the desired consistency. Store in a lidded container in the refrigerator for 1 week.

Uses
This sauce has a rich umami flavor to it, which makes it my favorite topper for any grain bowl. Serve with grilled or charred vegetables, a drizzle of sesame oil, and a sprinkle of sesame seeds.

Dishes
Grilled Squid, Green Tahini, and Chile Vinegar (page 243)

Roasted Eggplant Dip with Salsa Verde and Tahini (page 167)

Dragon Bowl (page 224)

Cashew Queso

MAKES 2 CUPS [400 G]

2 cups [250 g] cashews

2 cups [480 ml] boiling water

¾ cup [45 g] nutritional yeast

2 tsp ground turmeric

2 tsp salt

1 garlic clove

Put the cashews in a medium bowl and pour the boiling water over them until they are fully submerged. Allow them to soak for 15 minutes. Strain out the cashews, reserving the soaking liquid. Add the cashews, 1 cup [240 ml] of the soaking liquid, the yeast, turmeric, salt, and garlic to a high-powered blender. Blend for 2 minutes until it is smooth and resembles nacho cheese. If the blender is having a hard time processing, add a spoonful of water at a time until it reaches the desired consistency. Store in a lidded container in the refrigerator for 1 week.

Uses
Spread on toast and serve with pickles; add chopped jalapeño and use as a spicy dip; or add broth and chopped roasted or steamed broccoli and purée for a vegan broccoli cheese soup.

Dishes
Vegan Nachos (page 160)

Toast (page 169)

Romesco Sauce

MAKES 2½ CUPS [680 G]

½ cup [70 g] raw almonds

1 garlic clove

1 cup [225 g] jarred roasted red peppers, with their brine, stem and seeds removed

1¼ cups [300 ml] neutral oil, such as sunflower, grapeseed, safflower, or rice bran, or light olive oil

2 Tbsp sherry vinegar or red wine vinegar

¼ tsp salt

½ tsp smoked paprika

Pinch cayenne

In a food processor, pulse the almonds and garlic until well broken down. While the machine is still running, add the peppers and their brine, and process for 1 minute. Scrape the sides down with a rubber spatula. Slowly add the oil to emulsify—the sauce will become thick and smooth. Season with the vinegar, salt, smoked paprika, and cayenne, adding more as needed to please your palate. Store in a lidded container in the refrigerator for 1 week.

Uses

This sauce is traditionally served with calçots (grilled alliums) in Spain, but I like to add a few spoonfuls to risotto or a stew for flavor and body. You can also mix it with yogurt for a summer grill accompaniment.

Dish

Clams and Brothy Rice (page 245)

Peanut-Ginger Sauce

MAKES 1¼ CUPS [300 G]

2 garlic cloves

1 in [2.5 cm] piece ginger, peeled

2 Tbsp fresh lime juice

½ cup [130 g] crunchy or smooth peanut butter, sesame paste, or other nut butter (or a mix)

¼ cup [60 ml] hot filtered or spring water

3 Tbsp sesame oil

1 Tbsp soy sauce

1 tsp fish sauce or liquid aminos

2 tsp maple syrup

2 Tbsp tamarind paste (optional)

IF MAKING BY HAND: Mince or grate the garlic and ginger into a medium bowl. Add the lime juice and let sit for 5 minutes. In a separate bowl, add the peanut butter and hot water and whisk until smooth. Whisk in the sesame oil, soy sauce, fish sauce, maple syrup, tamarind paste (if using), and the lime mixture.

IF USING A BLENDER: Slice the ginger crosswise. Add all the ingredients to a high-speed blender and process for 45 seconds.

Store in a lidded container in the refrigerator for 1 week.

Uses

This sauce is great for crunchy salads or noodles paired with chopped peanuts or sesame seeds and Crispy Honey Chili Oil (page 118). Or use as a dip for chicken or tofu satay accompanied by a bright carrot salad.

Dishes

Chilled Noodles with Peanut-Ginger Sauce (page 200)

Dragon Bowl (page 224)

EGG-BASED SAUCES

When you think of egg-based sauces, the ones that come to mind are generally emulsifications such as mayonnaise, aioli, and hollandaise. In cooking, an emulsification is when two forces that don't usually mix combine into a molecular utopia similar to love. In order to make this happen, you must create the perfect environment in which each can be suspended within each other—complete unity. Be intentional and patient as you combine the ingredients. Note that mayo and aioli are two different things: Mayonnaise is made with white vinegar and a neutral oil, while aioli has minced garlic, uses lemon as its acidity, and is emulsified with a light-flavored olive oil. It takes technique to make emulsifications without breaking the sauce, so it's crucial to allow yourself some time to get the hang of it. If you master the process, these sauces can have a luxurious feel. The best part is that these sauces are blank canvases: You can throw in any number of ingredients, such as green olives into an aioli or pickled mustard seeds into a hollandaise, to add another dimension of flavor.

Mayonnaise Master Recipe

MAKES 1 CUP [240 G]

1 egg yolk, at room temperature

1 or 2 pinches sea salt

1 Tbsp white or white wine vinegar

¾ cup [180 ml] neutral oil, such as sunflower, grapeseed, safflower, or rice bran

In a bowl, add the egg yolk and salt and whisk for 5 seconds. Salt will cause a chemical reaction that will "cook" the eggs, so do not let it sit. Focus on the small bubbles that start to form within the egg, lightening the yolk. Add the vinegar and whisk for 1 minute. The frothy bubbles will start to cover the entire top of the egg mixture. Breathe deeply and slow down. The calmer and more methodical you are, the more success you will have.

While whisking constantly, use a spoon to start adding the oil slowly to the egg mixture. It will thicken and start becoming opaque, usually around the time a quarter of all the oil has been used, 2 minutes. Without breaking your focus, keep adding the oil a spoonful at a time until you've added all of it while continuing to whisk. It will turn to mayonnaise right before your eyes. Adjust the consistency by adding up to ½ teaspoon of water, a few droplets at a time, to loosen it a bit and add a lovely milkiness, like store-bought mayonnaise. Taste and adjust the salt or acidity to your preference.

If your sauce breaks, I recommend fixing it by starting with a new yolk and whisking in 1 tsp of Dijon mustard and 1 pinch of salt for 30 seconds and then slowly, spoon by spoon, adding in the broken mixture while whisking until completely combined.

For aioli style, you can use a mild olive oil as your oil and lemon juice instead of vinegar, and grate a garlic clove using a Microplane. Initially the garlic will read too strong, but it mellows after 5 minutes.

Store in a lidded container in the refrigerator for 5 days.

Green Olive or Caper Aioli

MAKES 1½ CUPS [360 G]

1 or 2 garlic cloves, sliced

½ tsp coarse sea salt

1 Tbsp fresh lemon juice

1 large egg yolk, at room temperature

¾ cup [180 ml] mild and fruity high-quality olive oil (taste your olive oil; if you find it too bitter, cut it with neutral oil by half)

½ cup [70 g] pitted and roughly chopped green olives or 2 Tbsp chopped capers (optional)

Using a mortar and pestle, make a paste with the garlic and salt (you can also use a Microplane to grate the garlic into a small bowl). Add the lemon juice and let it cure for a couple of minutes. Whisk in the yolk, then slowly add the oil as instructed in the Mayonnaise Master Recipe (left). Mix in olives or capers until fully combined.

Store in a lidded container in the refrigerator for 5 days.

Uses
Try this brinier, more flavorful variation of aioli as a sandwich spread or as a complement to a paella or tortilla Española.

Dishes
Salted Cod Puffs with Green Olive Aioli and Roasted Pecans (page 175)

Potatoes and Tomatoes with Tonnato (page 202)

Salt and Pepper Seafood Fry (page 251)

Hollandaise

MAKES ½ CUP [90 G]

1 egg yolk

1 Tbsp fresh lemon juice or vinegar

½ cup [110 g] clarified butter or ghee

¼ tsp salt

Pinch cayenne

In a bain-marie or a metal or glass bowl over a pot of low simmering water (ensure the bowl is not touching the water), whisk the egg yolk and the lemon juice together until thick, frothy, and light in color. While continuing to whisk, add the clarified butter in a very, very slow stream. Once all the butter has been whisked in, remove from the heat. Finish by adjusting the acidity, if needed, and then add the salt and a light sprinkle of cayenne. Keep covered and warm until ready to use. The consistency should be runny like a gravy. If it becomes too thick, whisk in hot water 1 tsp a time to loosen it.

If not using immediately, keep warm for up to 1 hour. Hollandaise cannot be cooled and reheated.

Uses
Hollandaise is one of my favorite sauces. It is rich and elevates any dish. It's so much more than a topper for the brunch standard of eggs Benedict; try it on fish, gnocchi, roasted potatoes, or steamed verdant spring vegetables.

Dish
Nigella Cauliflower Fritters with Pickled Mustard Seed Sauce (page 162)

Gribiche

MAKES 1 CUP [150 G]

½ cup [120 ml] extra-virgin olive oil

1 Tbsp vinegar

1 Tbsp whole-grain mustard

2 Tbsp chopped tart pickles

1 Tbsp capers, finely chopped

1 Tbsp pickle brine

1 tsp caper brine

Three 10-minute hard-boiled eggs, coarsely chopped

¼ cup [10 g] chopped soft herbs, such as parsley, chervil, chive, dill, or a mix

1 Tbsp Pickled Mustard Seed (optional, page 78)

In a medium bowl, whisk together the oil, vinegar, and mustard until emulsified. Add the pickles and capers along with their brines and stir to combine. Add the chopped eggs and stir to combine. Right before serving, add the chopped soft herbs and pickled mustard seed (if using).

Store in a lidded container in the refrigerator for 5 days.

Uses
Top toast with gribiche and salmon, serve it simply with boiled potatoes, or use it to accompany fish any style. I love it with peas and asparagus, especially in the spring months.

Dishes
Paprika Broth–Poached Striped Bass with Gribiche (page 250)

Toast (page 169)

Tonnato

MAKES 1¼ CUPS [300 G]

1 Tbsp vinegar or fresh lemon juice

2 whole anchovy fillets

½ cup [120 g] Mayonnaise Master Recipe (page 58)

5 to 7 oz [140 to 200 g] tuna packed in water or leftover cooked fish (see Note)

In a food processor or mixing bowl, add the vinegar and anchovy and let sit for a couple of minutes. Process or mash with a fork until the anchovies are broken down. Add the aioli and fish and pulse three or four times. Over-processing can break the sauce, turning the emulsification runny, so be sure to process until just combined. Use immediately or store in the refrigerator for 2 to 3 days.

NOTE: This recipe calls for high-quality tinned tuna, but seize the opportunity to use up any leftover cooked fish in the refrigerator to make this sauce.

Uses
This sauce is perfect with the season's peak tomatoes and thinly sliced onions, all topped with primo olive oil, or a summer char-grilled vegetable and fish dish. In the winter, try it with roasted vegetables and roasted spicy pumpkin seeds (see page 105).

Dishes
Potatoes and Tomatoes with Tonnato (page 202)

Crudo (page 236)

Eggless Caesar Dressing

MAKES 1½ CUPS [300 G]

1 garlic clove

3 Tbsp red wine or cider vinegar

8 oz [225 g] silken tofu

½ cup [120 ml] olive oil

1 lemon, juiced

2 anchovies (optional)

1½ tsp sea salt

1 tsp liquid aminos or fish sauce

1 tsp fresh ground black pepper

Using a Microplane, finely grate the garlic clove (or mash it). Place into a small food processor or blender. Add the vinegar and let cure for 10 minutes. Add the tofu, olive oil, lemon juice, anchovies (if using), salt, liquid aminos, and black pepper. Blend until smooth. Use immediately or store, refrigerated, for up to 3 days.

Uses
This is a great vegan dressing for a Caesar salad, a great dip for crudité, and a great sauce for a sandwich such as the Hippie Sandwich (page 153) or a tuna salad sandwich. Or use in a Niçoise bowl with potato, egg, poached fish, and green beans.

HERB SAUCES AND PESTOS

Pesto is more than just the traditional basil and pine nut sauce. Pesto, Italian for *pounded sauce*, lends itself to many different greens and vegetables. I believe that you can make a pesto out of almost anything: If you have leftover arugula, kale, parsley, greens, or even ramp leaves—a wild onion that generally grows around rivers with a life span of only three weeks—you can make a pesto. Think outside the box and experiment with adding kimchi, nori, or a little mint to give it another dimension. Pesto is not just for pasta—these pounded sauces provide added flavor to dressings and are great as dips on their own or added to yogurts.

Herb Sauce and Pesto Master Recipe

Here's a blueprint recipe for a simple herb and vegetable pesto that is made in a blender. Zucchini is a favorite; it blends to the consistency of a cream, as does leftover cooked broccoli. Using sad greens from the fridge like arugula and spinach is another great option.

MAKES 2 CUPS [225 G]

1½ cups [150 g] herbs or vegetables, roughly chopped

¼ cup [60 ml] light olive oil or a neutral oil, such as grapeseed or avocado

¼ cup [60 ml] lemon juice or vinegar

1 Tbsp flavor element, such as minced ginger or garlic, whole anchovy fillets, fish sauce, kimchi, preserved lemon, Flavor Paste (page 92), or ¼ cup [20 g] grated Parmesan or nutritional yeast

¼ tsp salt, plus more as needed

Black pepper

Chili powder, for serving

In a blender, add the herbs, oil, lemon juice, flavor element, and salt and blend on high speed for 1 minute. Add water a spoonful at a time to achieve the desired consistency. Season with salt, black pepper, and chili powder.

Use the same day, or store in a lidded container in the refrigerator for 3 days.

Pea Shoot Pesto

MAKES 1 CUP [220 G]

1 cup [40 g] pea tendrils, roughly chopped

2 whole anchovy fillets

1 Tbsp capers

1 Tbsp caper brine

¾ cup [180 ml] neutral oil, such as sunflower, grapeseed, safflower, or rice bran, or light-flavored olive oil

Add all the ingredients to a food processor and pulse until well combined.

Use the same day, or store in a lidded container in the refrigerator for 3 days.

Uses
Pea shoots and pea tendrils have an umami, almost cheese-like flavor when puréed. I like to leave the sauce a little chunky when serving with grilled vegetables and proteins, and blended smooth for dressings to drizzle over more delicate and raw vegetables. You can even add a swirl of it to a dip, like Green Tahini (page 54), for added richness and depth.

Dish
Wild Green Salad with Pea Shoot Pesto and Aged Pecorino (page 199)

Salsa Verde

MAKES 1½ CUPS [350 G]

1 garlic clove, sliced

2 whole anchovy fillets

1 cup [240 ml] mild extra-virgin olive oil or neutral oil, such as sunflower, grapeseed, safflower, or rice bran

½ cup [20 g] finely chopped parsley

¼ cup [10 g] finely chopped cilantro

¼ cup [10 g] finely chopped mint

2 Tbsp capers, chopped

1 Tbsp caper brine

1 Tbsp toasted and cracked coriander seeds (optional)

Juice of ½ lemon or 1 Tbsp preserved lemon purée

Zest of ½ lemon

In a medium-size mortar, mash the garlic and anchovy into a paste with a pestle. (If you don't have a large enough mortar, you can use a Microplane to grate the garlic into a small bowl and smash the anchovies with the side of a knife). Add the oil, parsley, cilantro, mint, capers, brine, coriander (if using), and lemon juice and zest and mix well.

Use the same day, or store in a lidded container in the refrigerator for 3 days.

Uses
This sauce works best with simple dishes like a plate of steamed vegetables or boiled baby potatoes, or with whole fish that has been steamed, salt baked, or grilled. It also works wonders drizzled on top of a dip like Green Tahini (page 54) or Beet–Sunflower Seed Sauce (page 53). You can make it like chunky relish by coarsely chopping the herbs and adding finely minced shallots or silky smooth by puréeing it in a blender. Any leftovers can be added to equal parts yogurt and avocado to make a quick version of Green Goddess Yogurt (page 39).

Dishes
Roasted Eggplant Dip with Salsa Verde and Tahini (page 167)

Salt-Baked Vegetables with Cacao Seed Mix (page 209)

Nori Pesto

MAKES 1 CUP [150 G]

¼ cup [35 g] pumpkin or sunflower seeds

¼ cup [60 ml] neutral oil, such as sunflower, grapeseed, safflower, or rice bran

3 sheets [10 g] nori, cut into 2 in [5 cm] pieces

1 cup [40 g] flat-leaf parsley, leaves only, no stems

2 Tbsp rice vinegar

¼ tsp salt

In a food processor, add the pumpkin seeds, oil, and nori and pulse to combine. Process for 30 seconds, making sure all the seeds have broken down. Add the parsley leaves. Process until it resembles a chunky pesto. Add the vinegar and salt and pulse for another 30 seconds until well incorporated.

Use the same day, or store in a lidded container in the refrigerator for 3 days.

Uses
This a great sauce to dab over a crudo, use as a dip for cold raw veggies (especially radishes), or to garnish a noodle bowl.

Dishes
Toast (page 169)

Crudo (page 236)

Walnut-Kimchi Dip

MAKES 2 CUPS [425 G]

½ cup [60 g] walnuts or pecans

½ cup [115 g] kimchi

½ cup [90 g] cooked white beans, such as chickpea or navy (optional, see Note)

¼ cup [67 g] chickpea miso or other mild miso

¼ cup [60 ml] apple cider vinegar or other light-colored vinegar

2 Tbsp tahini or nut butter

1 Tbsp maple syrup, honey, or agave

1 Tbsp fish sauce or liquid aminos (optional)

In a food processor, process the nuts and kimchi for 10 seconds. Add the beans (if using), miso, vinegar, tahini, maple syrup, and fish sauce (if using) and process for an additional 10 to 15 seconds, until combined.

Use the same day, or store in a lidded container in the refrigerator for 5 days.

NOTE: Adding beans to this sauce imparts a creaminess but, more importantly, allows you to use any leftover beans you may have on hand. This recipe is just as delicious with or without them.

Uses
This sauce has big flavor. Serve alongside simple summer vegetables or fritters for dipping or spread on a sandwich.

Dish
Grilled or Steamed Turnips and Their Greens with Walnut-Kimchi Dip (page 215)

Broccoli Pesto

MAKES 1½ CUPS [350 G]

1 cup [200 g] steamed or charred broccoli

½ cup [20 g] soft herbs, such as parsley, cilantro, sorrel, dill, or chervil

¼ cup [60 ml] extra-virgin olive oil

1 Tbsp lemon juice

1 Tbsp balsamic vinegar

¼ tsp salt

2 garlic cloves

1 Tbsp fish sauce or liquid aminos

1 tsp chopped jalapeño or Chile Paste (page 94)

¼ cup [20 g] nutritional yeast

Add all the ingredients to a food processor or blender and pulse until smooth. When using a blender, you may need to add a little water, a spoonful at a time to get the right consistency.

Use the same day, or store in a lidded container in the refrigerator for 3 days.

Uses
Want a great sauce for a summery pasta or grain salad? Need a way to take the leftover cooked vegetables from the fridge and give them new purpose? This is it.

Dish
Sprouted Whole Grains with Broccoli Pesto (page 231)

BUTTER SAUCES

Butter is a truly universal ingredient. It can become anything you want, from decadent sauces to molded centerpieces. Its inclusion in any meal adds an immediate touch of refinement and richness. Classic butter sauces, such as beurre blanc and beurre fondue, require whisking cold butter into a warm liquid to make an emulsion. Beurre blanc and beurre fondue are delicious, tangy, and decadent sauces. Beurre blanc is made with wine and butter and is often served with fish and vegetables. Beurre fondue uses broth and butter and is much lighter, used to poach fish and for warming delicate items such as blanched vegetables and gnocchi. Yes, these sauces do require technique, just like the egg emulsions, but it is worth the investment of your time to learn because there's so much you can do with them.

For a quicker, easier way to finish off a dish, I like having a few compound butters on hand—a dollop of butter atop any warm dish melts into a quick and luxurious sauce right before your eyes. You can add a bit of compound butter to toast or fresh radishes, add a spoonful to freshly sautéed vegetables, or use it to baste fish. Compound butter also shines in sweet applications: There is something special about mixing it with honey and turmeric and then adding it to a roasted sweet potato or even a tea cake. But my favorite way to use compound butter is to create a simple sauce by slowly simmering a bit of it with some tears of the gods (pasta cooking water) to create a decadent, silky coating for your pasta.

Quick Homemade Butter Master Recipe

MAKES 3 CUPS [520 G]

4 cups [960 ml] heavy cream

2 cups [80 g] soft herbs, such as parsley, chervil, and basil, or ½ cup [20 g] stronger herbs like rosemary or sage (optional, see Note)

2 tsp salt

Add the cream, herbs (if using), and salt to a food processor and process until the mixture starts to curdle and then separate, 3 to 4 minutes. What is left is butter and whey (or buttermilk if the milk had been cultured beforehand). Strain, saving the whey to use in place of liquid in soups, savory pancakes, baked goods, or even smoothies. Rinse the butter under cool water to remove any whey residue, as it can make your butter go rancid after a few days. Store in a glass or plastic container rolled into a log with parchment paper or in a mold for a special occasion. This will keep in the refrigerator for 1 month.

NOTE: This is a great way to use up excess herbs. When doing so, a food processor is the best way to go, as it breaks down the herbs and helps infuse the butter with their flavor.

Classic Butter Sauce

I prefer a butter sauce to be as light as possible, so this classic sauce is a mix of a beurre blanc and beurre fondue. Like the mayonnaise from page 58, this sauce is an emulsion, so all elements need to be treated with care to prevent the sauce from breaking.

MAKES 1 CUP [240 ML]

½ cup [120 ml] white wine

½ shallot, thickly sliced

½ cup [110 g] butter, cut into cubes and chilled

Add the wine and shallots to a small pot over medium heat. Slowly bring up to a simmer and continue simmering for 5 minutes, or until the liquid reduces by half. Remove from the heat. Using a slotted spoon or tongs, remove the shallots (toss in a salad). Add ¼ cup [60 ml] or enough water to the wine mixture to make ½ cup [120 ml]. Return the pot to low heat and bring the liquid back up to a light simmer.

While whisking rapidly and continuously, begin adding about a quarter of the cold butter to the pot. Butter melts and separates at 158°F [70°C], so do not allow your smooth, luscious sauce to get too hot, or it will break. As the butter begins to melt, whisk in a few pieces of the remaining butter at a time. After all of the butter has been added, remove from the heat and whisk until every piece of butter has melted into the sauce.

Keep covered in a warm spot until ready to serve. You can save any leftovers in the refrigerator for 2 weeks, but be sure to use a double boiler to reheat, stirring often, or your emulsion will break.

Uses
In my opinion, there is nothing more decadent than this rich, tart sauce served alongside a platter of the finest steamed summer vegetables. It also makes a beautiful sauce for gnocchi— gently slide just-simmered gnocchi into a pot of this sauce to bathe for a minute or so, plate, and finish with a squeeze of lemon and a sprinkle of chili powder.

Dish
Poached Prawns in Mustard Seed Butter Sauce (page 246)

Avocado-Cumin Butter

MAKES 1 CUP [220 G]

½ cup [110 g] butter, ghee, or coconut oil, at room temperature

1 avocado, peeled and pitted

1 tsp ground cumin

1 tsp lemon juice

Salt

Add the butter, avocado, cumin, and lemon juice to a food processor and season with salt. Process until the avocado has broken all the way down. Shape into a log or transfer to a lidded container. Store in the refrigerator for 1 week.

Uses
Use a dollop and a sprinkle of seeds on avocado toast or add to a dal or other stew to impart richness.

Dish
Flatbread with Spiced Oil and Everything Dukkah Mix or with Avocado Butter, Cumin, and Sesame Condiment (page 138)

Miso Butter

MAKES 1¼ CUPS [290 G]

1 cup [220 g] butter or ghee, at room temperature

¼ cup [67 g] chickpea miso or other light miso

1 Tbsp sesame butter or tahini

Add all the ingredients to a medium bowl and mix well. Shape into a log and roll in parchment paper or transfer to a lidded container. Store it in the refrigerator for 3 months.

Uses

My favorite use for this is on a whole roasted sweet potato sprinkled with a sesame mix, but it's also delicious melted on a toasted slice of cornbread or tender loaves such as brioche and milk bread. It's also great for cooking glazed carrots or for finishing off sautéed mushrooms.

Dish

Savory Oat and Rice Porridge (page 129)

Uni Butter

MAKES ¾ CUP [165 G]

10 lobes uni (see Note)

½ cup [110 g] salted butter, at room temperature

1 tsp fresh lemon juice

¼ tsp sea salt

Small pinch cayenne pepper or chili powder

In a food processor, add the uni and process for a few seconds. Add the butter, lemon juice, salt, and cayenne and process until smooth. Shape into a log and roll in parchment paper or transfer to a lidded container. Store it in the refrigerator for 2 weeks.

NOTE: Uni, or sea urchin, can be found at local fish markets or Asian grocers. It is always used fresh.

Uses

Spread it on toasted fluffy bread like brioche, challah, or milk bread. Coat warm linguini with the butter, adding some tears of the gods (a.k.a. pasta water) to turn it into a creamy uni sauce. Serve it on top of warm vegetables or fish so it melts slowly. This butter should not be used to cook with, as it can turn fishy fast.

Dish

Toast (page 169)

Cinnamon Turmeric Honey Ghee

MAKES ½ CUP [110 G]

½ cup [110 g] room-temperature ghee, butter, or coconut oil

2 Tbsp honey

½ tsp ground cinnamon

¼ tsp ground turmeric

¼ tsp salt

Add all the ingredients to a small bowl and mix well. Shape into a log or transfer to a lidded container. Store in the refrigerator for 1 month.

Uses

Spread on toast, biscuits, pancakes, or waffles or dollop it on porridges or roasted sweet potatoes. It's also great frothed into warm milk at a ratio of 1 or 2 tsp cold butter per 1 cup [240 ml] warm milk.

Dish

Warm Carrot-Almond Tea Cake with Cinnamon Turmeric Honey Ghee (page 146)

PICKLES, FERMENTS, AND CURES

Pickling, fermenting, and curing are methods of preserving ingredients, with the added benefit of being great for gut health. Pickles are made by allowing an ingredient to sit in a vinegar solution. Fermentation is achieved by adding salt to an item and allowing it to sit exposed to nature's beneficial bacteria so that the item releases its water, leaving behind a natural briny pickling solution. Fermentation is the process by which we create kimchi, sour pickles, and sauerkraut. It is an ancient practice to eat them alongside rich dishes to aid in digestion of the meal as a whole. Cures are exclusively for fish and meats, extending their shelf life but also giving the item a denser consistency. Adding lemon or vinegar to garlic so it's easier on the palate also counts as curing.

Pickling Solution Master Recipe

MAKES ¾ CUP [180 ML], OR ENOUGH SOLUTION FOR 1 PINT [480 G] OF PICKLES

This solution is easy to adapt for any amount of vegetables. You can scale up or down with a basic ratio: Starting with the amount of vinegar, halve that amount to get the water measurement, and then halve the water measurement to get the sugar measurement.

½ cup [120 ml] vinegar of your choice

¼ cup [60 ml] filtered or spring water

2 Tbsp sweetener, such as organic honey, agave, maple syrup, or cane sugar

2 Tbsp salt

ADD-INS (OPTIONAL)

Hearty aromatics, such as sliced garlic or onion

Whole, dried, or fresh chiles

Woody herbs, such as bay and thyme

Whole spices, such as coriander, mustard, and fennel seeds

Add the vinegar, water, sweetener, and salt to a medium pot over medium heat. Bring to a simmer, stir until all the sugar is melted and incorporated, and remove from the heat. Add raw vegetables to a clean jar with a lid and pour the brine over the vegetables, making sure they are submerged. For denser items like carrots, use brine while hot to help poach them slightly. For more tender vegetables, like sliced cucumber or onions, allow the brine to come to room temperature before using. If you're using tender and/or sliced vegetables and no whole spices, you can add all the pickling ingredients to a medium bowl and whisk together to combine—no heating required before adding to the vegetables.

Refrigerate and allow the vegetables to pickle for at least 2 hours before using, though overnight is best. They will keep in a lidded container in the refrigerator for 1 month.

After you've used up the vegetables from the first pickle, you can use the leftover pickling liquid for one more batch. Bring it to a simmer along with an additional splash of vinegar, and then follow the instructions above.

Cucumber and Dulse Pickle

MAKES 2 CUPS [400 G]

1 unwaxed cucumber, thinly sliced

¼ cup [14 g] dulse or wakame seaweed

1 recipe Pickling Solution Master Recipe (left) using rice vinegar and cane sugar, at room temperature

2 Tbsp cane sugar

Add the sliced cucumber and dulse to a medium jar and pour the pickling solution over. Refrigerate and allow the vegetables to pickle for at least 2 hours before using, though overnight is best. They will keep in the refrigerator for 1 week.

Uses
This makes a wonderful topping for dressed rice, a sliced fresh shiso leaf, and Gomasio (page 105), or a grain bowl.

Dish
Dragon Bowl (page 224)

Chile-Mushroom Pickle

MAKES 2 CUPS [440 G]

2 Tbsp olive oil, plus more for topping

8 oz [230 g] small whole mushrooms, such as honey or beech

2 fresh or dried small chiles, whole or thinly sliced, or 1 tsp Chile Paste (page 94)

½ shallot, thinly sliced

1 recipe Pickling Solution Master Recipe (page 76)

Add the oil to a medium pan over medium heat and sauté the mushrooms. Do not salt the mushrooms, as it can cause them to lose moisture. If they seem to be browning but are not yet tender, add 1 Tbsp of water to the pan and quickly place a lid over them, turn the heat to low, and allow them to steam.

Transfer to a clean medium jar, add the chiles and shallot, and pour the pickling solution over. For extra richness, you can top with up to 2 Tbsp additional oil, such as olive or sesame. Refrigerate and allow to pickle for at least 2 hours before using, though overnight is best. They will keep in the refrigerator for 2 weeks.

Uses
I love these as a topping on cheesy toast, in a sandwich, on a snack plate for apéro hour, or in a salmon and rice bowl.

Dishes
Toast (page 169)

Maple Chicories with Chile-Mushroom Pickle (page 168)

Dried Red Berry and Beet Pickle

MAKES 1½ CUPS [330 G]

1 small beet, peeled and grated

½ cup [70 g] dried red berries, such as goji berries, barberries, or cherries

10 thin slices fresh ginger

1 recipe Pickling Solution Master Recipe (page 76) using red wine vinegar, hot

Fill a clean medium jar with the beets, dried berries, and sliced ginger. Add the hot pickling solution and let cool. Refrigerate and allow to pickle for at least 2 hours before using, though overnight is best. They will keep in the refrigerator for 2 weeks.

Uses
This pickle has always been the crown jewel in my restaurant grain bowls, and it makes a great garnish for any dish that needs a pop of color and acidity. You can reuse this pickling solution to pickle eggs: Boil the solution, cool slightly, add hard- or medium-boiled eggs, and let them sit overnight in the fridge for bright pink and delicious eggs.

Dishes
Collard Green and Peach Summer Salad (page 193)

Dragon Bowl (page 224)

Pickled Mustard Seed

MAKES ¾ CUP [160 G]

¼ cup [50 g] mustard seeds

½ cup [120 ml] Pickling Solution Master Recipe (page 76), hot

In a small pot, add the mustard seeds and 1 cup [240 ml] filtered water. Bring to a boil and drain, discarding the liquid. Repeat this process two times more. After the last drain, add the mustard seeds to a small, clean jar. Add the hot pickling solution and let cool. Refrigerate and allow to pickle for at least 2 hours before using, though overnight is best. They will keep in the refrigerator for 1 month.

Uses
This is an ideal finishing element for prepared dishes, such as avocado toast, tartines, salads, and composed vegetable dishes. Add it to a fruit conserve for a quick chutney, or incorporate it into heavier sauces such as Hollandaise (page 59) or Mayonnaise (page 58) to dress them up a bit.

Dishes
Nigella Cauliflower Fritters with Pickled Mustard Seed Sauce (page 162)

Poached Prawns in Mustard Seed Butter Sauce (page 246)

Gribiche (page 59)

Dragon Bowl (page 224)

Pickled Dried Fruit

MAKES 1 CUP [200 G]

½ cup [70 to 90 g] dried fruit, such as figs, apricots, and raisins

1 recipe Pickling Solution Master Recipe (page 76), hot

Add the dried fruit to a clean medium jar. Add the hot pickling solution and let cool. Refrigerate and allow to pickle overnight for the fruit to reconstitute. They will keep in a lidded container in the refrigerator for 2 weeks.

Uses
These plump and tart fruit pickles are extremely pleasing chopped and served over roasted autumn squashes or with a chicory salad.

Dishes
Crudo (page 236)

Ferment Master Recipe

YIELD VARIES

Weight of vegetable x 0.02 = weight of sea salt (for every 50 g of vegetable, use 1 tsp of sea salt)

If you're new to fermenting, start with sliced cabbage, fennel, and chiles, as they are the easiest to make. Use gloves for handling chiles.

Thinly slice the vegetables and weigh them, using the formula above to determine the amount of salt.

In a large bowl, combine the vegetables and salt, massaging the salt into the vegetables until they start to release their water.

Pack the vegetables and their liquid into a sterile jar. Add fermenting weights to the jar to push down the vegetables until they're completely submerged. (Fermenting weights are glass weights that help push down the vegetables to eliminate exposure to air that allows for bacteria growth.) If the vegetables do not yield enough liquid to cover, you can make a saline solution by dissolving 1 Tbsp sea salt in 1 cup [240 ml] filtered or spring water. Add 1 Tbsp of the solution at a time until the brine covers the vegetables. Cover with a lid. Store at room temperature away from direct sunlight. I don't like putting it in the cupboard because I risk forgetting it.

Remove the lid every day to release any gas (this process is called burping). After 2 days, taste the vegetables—they should be tangy. If not, keep it out for another day. If you approve of its tartness, move it to the refrigerator. The ferment keeps for 1 month in the refrigerator in a lidded container.

Turmeric, Fennel, and Onion Condiment

MAKES 1 CUP [150 G]

1½ cups [150 g] sliced fennel

¼ cup [35 g] sliced onion

1 tsp salt

½ tsp ground turmeric

Add the fennel and onion to a large bowl, and add the salt. Use your hands to massage the salt into the vegetables until they start to release their water. Mix in the turmeric with a spoon so that your hands do not stain. Pack, ferment, and store according to the process described in Ferment Master Recipe (left).

Uses
This makes a great topping for spicy curries, vegetable or fish sandwiches, or any grain bowl.

Dishes
Vegan Nachos (page 160)

Hippie Sandwich (page 153)

Red Cabbage and Nigella Relish

MAKES 2 CUPS [400 G]

2 cups [300 g] red cabbage

½ large red onion, finely chopped

½ cup [120 ml] red wine vinegar or fresh lemon juice

2 tsp toasted nigella seeds

Ferment the cabbage according to the process described in the Ferment Master Recipe (page 79).

Once fermented, in a large bowl, add the onion and the vinegar to cover. Let sit for 15 minutes. In a food processor, add the fermented cabbage and process until it is the same size as the onion. Mix the cabbage and nigella seeds into the onion mixture. Transfer to a medium jar, cover tightly, and store in the refrigerator for 1 to 2 months.

Uses
This relish is a great accompaniment to a fritter or in a vegetable sandwich.

Dish
Toast (page 169)

Fermented Hot Sauce

MAKES 2 CUPS [480 ML]

2 lb [910 g] fresh red chiles, such as Thai bird or Fresno

1½ Tbsp kosher, Himalayan, or sea salt, plus more for seasoning

Using gloves, remove the stems from the chiles and ferment with the salt according to the process described in the Ferment Master Recipe (page 79). Once fermented, pulse in a blender until smooth. Store in a lidded container in the refrigerator for 1 year.

Uses
This sauce is basically great on everything that calls for some heat and acid, such as egg and bean burritos, rice and beans, and sandwiches. Pick up 2 lb [910 g] of fresh chiles when they are in season at the market; you'll make a big enough batch to last you all year. Get double that and make enough to gift.

Dish
Corn and Black Sesame Tamales (page 219)

Fish Cure Master Recipe

MAKES ¾ CUP [120 G]

This basic cure recipe is easy to adapt for any amount of fish. You can scale up or down using the basic formula of 1 part aromatics to 4 parts sugar to 8 parts salt.

½ cup [65 g] kosher salt

¼ cup [50 g] sugar

1 Tbsp aromatics (see Note)

2 lb [910 g] fish fillets, such as salmon or fluke

In a large bowl, mix together the salt, sugar, and aromatics. If using fresh herbs, cut them into the salt and sugar using a food processor or knife. Line the counter with parchment paper or plastic wrap. Place the fish fillet skin-side down, top with the cure, and pack it tightly. Wrap the fish completely with the paper or plastic wrap. Place on a rack with a sheet pan underneath to catch any liquid the fish releases. Cure in the refrigerator for 1 or 2 days depending on the size of the fish. Remove the fish from its wrap and wipe off the cure completely using a paper towel and discard, along with any liquid. Slice thin and serve. The fish will keep in the refrigerator for 2 weeks.

NOTE: Aromatics include whole spices such as juniper; herbs such as thyme, rosemary, lavender flower, fresh lavender leaf, and dill; and fruits and vegetables such as citrus zest and freshly grated beets.

Lavender Salt Cure

MAKES 1½ CUPS [240 G]

1 cup [130 g] kosher salt

½ cup [100 g] granulated cane sugar

2 Tbsp finely chopped fresh lavender leaves or 1 Tbsp dried lavender flowers

2 lb [910 g] salmon fillet, or another fatty fish

Follow the instructions for the Fish Cure Master Recipe (left) using the lavender as your aromatic. If using fish that is leaner than salmon, cut the curing time in half. The cured fish will keep for 1 week in the refrigerator, while the cure mix can last for 1 month.

Uses
This works well with other fatty fish such as Arctic char. You can use citrus zest in place of the lavender.

Dish
Toast (page 169)

Kombu Cure

MAKES ENOUGH FOR 1 LB [455 G] FISH

1 large sheet kombu

¼ cup [60 ml] mirin

1 Tbsp vinegar

1 Tbsp soy sauce

1 lb [455 g] fish fillet, such as tuna, fluke, or bass

Line the counter with plastic wrap or parchment paper. Using scissors, cut the sheet of kombu in half. Place one half of the kombu on top of the plastic or parchment. In a medium bowl, mix together the mirin, vinegar, and soy sauce. Dip the fish into the mirin mixture, remove, and place it directly on the kombu. Place the other half of the kombu on top of the fish and wrap tightly in the plastic wrap or parchment paper. Place on a plate and cure in the refrigerator for 2 hours or overnight. Unwrap the fish and discard the kombu sheets. The cured fish will keep in the refrigerator for an additional 1 to 2 days.

Uses

This is a traditional Japanese way of curing fish, and it can be used in many raw fish applications or served with a simple bowl of steamed rice and pickles.

Dish

Kombu-Cured Fish with Quinoa-Potato Crisp (page 240)

STOCKS, BROTHS, AND DASHIS

In 1765, a Parisian named Boulanger once said, "Come to me all who suffer from pain of the stomach, and I will restore you." He opened a shop specializing in restorative concentrated broths, advertised as an antidote to physical exhaustion. The shop was called a *restaurant*, a place to "restaurare," or renew or restore. Over the years, the word *restaurant* has become a worldwide term for all eating establishments. Boulanger was on to something.

Stock is great to have on hand to sip for restoring yourself—and to use in many recipes. When you get into the routine of making it, you'll never be without it. Use it to give depth to risotto and soups, in a garlicky wine sauce for pasta, or, my favorite, for steaming leafy greens such as chicories or smaller cabbages such as bok choy and then serving them with the broth as a sauce. Broths have a concentration of minerals that

are beneficial, too. Because I try to utilize everything I can from my market ingredients, I save all the scraps—onion ends, carrot skins, corn cobs, garlic skins—and when I have enough, I make a broth out of them by adding peppercorn, bay leaf, and other spices. I season it with tamari if I want to make it a sipping broth. Making a rich broth is a great way to see the payoff from the bits of cooking scraps you've collected over a couple of weeks.

Stock Master Recipe

AT LEAST 1 PART SOLIDS (SEE NOTE) TO 2 PARTS COOL FILTERED OR SPRING WATER

Always start stocks in cold water to extract the most flavor. In a large pot, combine the solids and the water. Place over low heat and bring to a simmer over the course of 1 hour. Simmer for at least 4 hours or up to 12 hours for denser solids such as bones. I like to start a stock in the afternoon, turn it off before I go to sleep, let it cool overnight, then bring it back up to a gentle simmer for an additional few hours in the morning. Cool and strain. Pull a pint or a quart to stash in the freezer for future steamed greens, ramen, or morning miso soup on a cold day.

NOTE: Solids can be anything from whole or scraps of vegetables, herbs, roots, spices, and bones—sometimes I even toss in an apple core. I like to collect solids in the freezer until I have around 4 cups [600 g].

Toasted Barley– Seaweed–Bonito Dashi

MAKES 4 CUPS [960 ML]

5 cups [1.2 L] cool filtered or spring water

½ onion, cut into 4 pieces

10 dried shiitake mushrooms

4 in [10 cm] piece kombu

3 Tbsp whole mugicha (toasted barley tea)

2 Tbsp bonito flakes

In a medium pot, add the water, onion, mushrooms, kombu, and mugicha. Bring to a simmer—do not boil. After 30 to 45 minutes over low heat, remove the kombu from the broth, reserving for another use (see Note). Set up a strainer over a bowl. Stir the bonito into the pot and simmer for 15 seconds. Strain. This keeps in a lidded container in the refrigerator for 1 week.

NOTE: The mushroom caps and kombu can be sliced thin and added to soups or salads (it's great with Honey-Miso Dressing, page 45). The strained barley tea can also be reused— you can add it to a sipping broth or use it as a garnish for steamed greens in broth.

Uses

I like to have this dashi on hand at all times, as it's a versatile broth with a toasted, earthy note. I use it for miso soup, noodle soup, or in a soup of puréed winter squash.

Dish

Dragon Bowl (page 224)

Coconut-Ginger Broth

MAKE 4 CUPS [960 ML]

1 Tbsp coconut oil

1 medium onion, coarsely chopped

1 lemongrass stalk, tough outer layers removed, slightly smashed

2 in [5 cm] piece ginger, thinly sliced, or 2 Tbsp Fresh Curry Paste (page 94)

½ tsp Himalayan pink or sea salt

¼ cup [60 ml] white wine

2 cups [480 ml] cool filtered or spring water

One 13½ oz [385 g] can unsweetened coconut milk

Heat the oil in a large pot over medium-low heat. Add the onion, lemongrass, ginger, and salt. Cover and cook for approximately 10 minutes, checking and stirring to make sure no browning occurs. Add the wine and simmer for 5 minutes. Add the water and coconut milk. Simmer for 20 minutes more. Strain, discarding the solids. The broth keeps in a lidded container in the refrigerator for 1 week.

Uses

This is a satisfying broth for steaming mussels or clams. Start with sautéing a power paste (see page 92). Once it begins to sizzle, add the mussels or clams and broth, cover, and simmer over low heat until the shells open up.

Dish

Squash with Peanut-Coconut Curry (page 217)

Corn and Parmesan Broth

MAKES 6 CUPS [1.4 L]

8 cups [2 L] cool filtered or spring water

1 lb [455 g] Parmesan cheese rinds (see Note)

6 corn cobs and their silk (see Note)

1 onion, thinly sliced

1 head garlic, sliced crosswise

Sea salt

In a large pot over low heat, add the water, Parmesan rinds, corn cobs and silk, onion, and garlic. Bring to a simmer, then simmer for 2 hours. Strain and adjust the seasoning with salt. This broth keeps in a lidded container in the refrigerator for 1 week and in the freezer for 6 months.

NOTE: Stow away your Parmesan rinds and summer corn cobs and silk in the freezer until you have enough for this broth.

Uses

This is one of my favorite broths. Its use of rinds and cobs, elements we normally throw away, impart big flavor. You'll love it in a simple vegetable and pasta soup, but it's also delicious as a base for a risotto.

Dishes

Fresh Corn Polenta with Corn and Parmesan Broth (page 220)

Corn and Potato Chowder (page 221)

Turmeric-Ginger-Chile Vegetable Broth or Consommé

MAKES 4 CUPS [960 ML]

6 cups [1.4 L] cool filtered or spring water

2 to 3 cups [300 to 450 g] thinly sliced vegetables, such as onions, onion skins, garlic, carrots, celery, mushrooms, and herb stems (see Note)

6 dried chiles de árbol or your favorite dried chile

3 in [7.5 cm] piece fresh ginger

2 in [5 cm] piece fresh turmeric

2 Tbsp chickpea miso or other light-colored miso

FOR CONSOMMÉ

1 cup [150 g] minced onion, celery, and carrots or vegetable juicer scraps

3 egg whites

To make the vegetable broth: In a large pot over medium heat, combine the water, sliced vegetables, chiles, ginger, turmeric, and miso. Bring to a simmer and simmer over low heat for 2 to 6 hours—this broth favors a long, slow simmer. Strain. You can use as is or make your broth into a consommé.

To make the broth into a consommé: Start by chilling the broth for at least 2 hours or overnight. In a medium pot, combine the cold broth, minced vegetables, and egg whites. Bring to a simmer. Cook over low heat, stirring every few minutes, for 20 minutes. After 20 minutes, stop stirring and allow a raft of the egg white mixture to form. The egg whites will attract and stick to particles and impurities from the broth to give you a clarified consommé. Be careful not to boil at this point, or the raft will break. After an additional 20 minutes, line a strainer with two layers of cheesecloth and make a hole in the center of the raft with your ladle. Carefully ladle out the broth from the center into the strainer, trying your best not to disturb the raft. The consommé keeps in a lidded container in the refrigerator for 2 weeks.

NOTE: Leafy greens and herbs are not good for this recipe, as they'll make the broth very dark.

Uses
This recipe makes a great base for soup or can be enjoyed on its own as a simple and nourishing sipping broth. I love to see it served with baby tortellini as in Italy. The consommé version is perfect served with steamed baby vegetables or dumplings.

Dishes
Squash with Peanut-Coconut Curry (page 217)

Plantain Dumpling Stew (page 216)

FLAVOR PASTES

These may be some of the most valuable ingredients to keep in your refrigerator. And to prove it is to know every old-world cuisine has a foundational flavor base that is often created from herbs and aromatics. While some, such as French mirepoix and Italian sofritto, are comprised of finely chopped vegetables, others blend the chiles and spices together to make what I like to call flavor pastes: Latin America has sofrito, there is the "holy trinity" in the African American South, Cambodia has kroeung, and the list goes on. I always like to have a few different pastes on hand because they're super beneficial in developing a deep, delicious flavor in beans, soups, stews, and more. Some flavor pastes, such as sofrito, are added early on in the cooking process because they benefit from a quick fry to bloom the flavors before adding the main ingredients, though curing a paste in vinegar or lemon and adding it to a dressing is a quick hack. Other pastes, such as miso, preserved lemon purée, tamarind, mole paste, and Marmite, are traditionally added toward the end of the cooking process to bring dimension to the flavor and balance the dish.

Flavor Paste Master Recipe

MAKES ¾ CUP [145 G]

This is great for winter, when you need these strong and healthy ingredients to keep immunity up. Save herb stems for this—they have great flavor.

1 head garlic, cloves peeled

2 shallots, peeled

2 in [5 cm] piece fresh turmeric, peeled

½ cup [10 g] chopped cilantro stems

Add all the ingredients to a small food processor or mortar and pulse or mash into a paste. To use, sauté in 1 to 2 Tbsp of oil as a base for soups, beans, or sauces. This paste keeps in the refrigerator for 2 months or in the freezer for 6 months.

Summer Sofrito, Recaito Any Other Time

MAKES 2 CUPS [380 G]

1 Spanish onion, quartered

1 green bell pepper or Cubanelle, cored and quartered

1 tomato (if tomatoes are out of season, omit)

1 jalapeño, seeded

1 bunch cilantro or culantro (saw-leaf herb), cut into 1 in [2.5 cm] pieces (see Note)

5 garlic cloves

Add all the ingredients to a food processor or blender and purée until the texture is that of a loose paste. If using a blender, add a bit of water a little at a time to help nudge it along if it gets stuck. This paste keeps in a lidded container in the refrigerator for 2 months or in the freezer for 6 months.

NOTE: Sofrito is traditionally made with culantro, an herb that has a similar aroma and flavor to cilantro, but has much more intensity. It's usually used to cook with and rarely served raw as a garnish. Without the tomato, sofrito is called *recaito*. My philosophy is that I eat fresh produce only when it's in season, so I will make sofrito only during the summer months when tomatoes are at their peak.

Uses

The jalapeño in this recipe is not traditional but it lends more dimension. This is a base for many dishes all over the world, but this particular recipe is one from my maternal family with roots in Puerto Rico. Use it as a base for stock, beans in their liquid, stews, and soups.

Dishes

Cuban Beans, Coconut Rice, and Steamed Sweet Plantains (page 212)

Plantain Dumpling Stew (page 216)

Corn and Black Sesame Tamales (page 219)

Chile Paste

MAKES 1 CUP [240 G]

1 lb [455 g] fresh spicy and sweet red chiles

Aromatics, such as fish sauce, fresh herbs, ginger, or ground cumin (optional)

Remove the stems from the peppers. Seeding the peppers is optional depending on your heat preference—eventually the heat subsides a bit, so I always leave them in. Add the chiles and aromatics (if using) to a food processor or blender and pulse until finely chopped. Store any leftovers in a lidded container in the freezer for 6 months.

Uses

I like to make this quick paste in the summer when fresh chiles and peppers are abundant. Freeze a little bit for the winter when you need some fire to take out a cold. It also makes a great finisher for a crudo dressing or mixed with lime and salt to offer as a condiment when a chile connoisseur comes over for dinner. Fresh chiles are fruity, so when I'm ready to cook with this paste, I like mixing it with dried chiles in stews, curries, or sautés to deepen the flavor.

Dishes

Squash with Peanut-Coconut Curry (page 217)

Turmeric Lentil Rice with Mustard and Cumin Seeds (page 233)

Chile-Mushroom Pickle (page 77)

Broccoli Pesto (page 65)

Crudo (page 236)

Fresh Curry Paste

MAKES ½ CUP [120 G]

3 lemongrass stalks, outer tough layers removed, thinly sliced

1 jalapeño or other green chile [about 25 g], seeded depending on heat preference and coarsely chopped

3 in [7.5 cm] piece ginger, peeled and thinly sliced crosswise

1 in [2.5 cm] piece fresh turmeric, peeled (optional)

1 Tbsp fish sauce or liquid aminos

Using a food processor or mortar and pestle, process all the ingredients together until a smooth paste forms. Add water a spoonful at a time if necessary to reach the right consistency. This paste keeps in a lidded container in the refrigerator for 2 months or in the freezer for 6 months.

Uses

This curry paste is key as a base for curries, soups, and stews. Sauté a bit of the paste and use it as a base for shellfish, such as large prawns or mussels. Add wine, broth, or coconut milk for saucy preparations. Add lime zest, curry leaves, or lime leaves for more complex variations.

Dishes

Squash with Peanut-Coconut Curry (page 217)

Coconut-Ginger Broth (page 87)

Carrot Harissa

MAKES 1 CUP [230 G]

1 lb [455 g] carrots, cut into 1 in [2.5 cm] slices (see Note)

½ onion, thinly sliced

1 Tbsp grapeseed oil

1 tsp honey, maple syrup, or agave

1 tsp salt

2 tsp paprika

¼ tsp ground turmeric

¼ tsp ground cumin

¼ tsp ground coriander

¼ tsp chili powder

1 tsp preserved lemon purée, or 1 Tbsp lemon juice and a few scrapes of lemon zest

Preheat the oven or toaster oven to 350°F [180°C]. Line a baking sheet with parchment paper.

Spread the carrots and onion on the prepared baking sheet, drizzle with the oil, honey, and salt, and roast for 30 minutes. Toss, and roast for an additional 30 minutes until tender. Sprinkle with the paprika, turmeric, cumin, coriander, and chili powder and toss. Roast for 3 minutes more.

Remove from the oven and allow to cool. Transfer the mixture to a food processor or blender, making sure to capture all the remaining spices with a rubber spatula. Add the lemon purée and process until smooth. If it's not processing with ease, nudge it along by adding 1 Tbsp of water at a time while the machine is running. This can take up to 2 minutes until you have a smooth orange purée. This keeps in a lidded container in the refrigerator for 1 week.

NOTE: You can substitute carrots for other orange vegetables, such as sweet potatoes, winter squash, or rutabaga, or go traditional with roasted and peeled red peppers.

Uses

Add 2 Tbsp to a soup base or spread on fish prior to cooking. Combine with ½ cup [120 g] strained yogurt and a bit of salt to taste to make a dipping sauce for flatbread, for a Dragon Bowl (page 224), or as a dressing for a crunchy cabbage slaw.

Dish

Turmeric Lentil Rice with Mustard and Cumin Seeds (page 233)

FRUIT SAUCES AND TONICS

To create a perfectly balanced flavor, you need a touch of sweet, and fruit sauces are great for adding a sweet note to dishes. I use four main fruit sauces in my cooking: compotes, jams, molasses, and tonics. Compotes are dried or fresh fruits that are left whole or in large pieces and poached in a light syrup. Jams are comprised of crushed or chopped fruits that are cooked down in sugar and their own juices until reduced to a spreadable consistency. For the purposes of this book, a molasses is a jam that is reduced to a very thick consistency. And tonics are a slightly fermented mix of fruit, sugar, and vinegar with a loose syrup consistency.

Most dishes rely on a balance of salty, tart, sweet, and spicy. When the fruit in the summer is abundant, I like to grab up as much as possible and make some fruit sauces to use throughout the year. Because I'm all about no waste, it's also a great way to utilize extra fruit that you have at its peak. Some of my favorites are apricot, plum, and cranberry, and I like pairing these sweet items with savory dishes to make them pop. You can also lend a touch of sweetness by adding bits to a vinaigrette, or just swirl them on their own into porridge and oatmeal.

Compote Master Recipe

MAKES 2 CUPS [600 G]

1 lb [455 g] fresh fruit, such as pitted stone fruit (peaches, apricots, and plums); berries (blueberries, cranberries, and currants); whole figs; pears and apples, peeled, cored, and cut into large bite-size pieces; or rhubarb

Aromatics, such as cinnamon stick, cardamom pod, or a slice of fresh ginger

1 cup [240 ml] filtered or spring water

2 to 4 Tbsp [30 to 60 ml] organic natural sweetener, such as maple syrup, honey, agave, or cane sugar

In a small pot over low heat, add the fruit, aromatics, water, and 2 Tbsp of the sweetener. Let the mixture come to a gentle simmer. Simmer dried fruits for 5 minutes or fresh apples, pears, figs, and stone fruits for 5 to 10 minutes, until tender. For delicate fruits like rhubarb and berries, it's better to poach off the flame. For rhubarb, cut into 2 in [5 cm] pieces, turn off the heat, and add to the warm poaching liquid. Cover and let sit for 5 minutes until tender. For berries like raspberries and blackberries, turn off the heat, then add the whole berries to the warm poaching liquid. Let sit, uncovered, for 1 to 2 minutes until tender.

Add any extra sweetener to taste. This compote keeps in a lidded container in the refrigerator for 3 days.

Fruit Jam or Molasses Master Recipe

MAKES 2 CUPS [600 G]

2 cups [about 300 g] peeled and pitted fresh fruit, chopped if using large fruit

¼ to ½ cup [50 to 100 g] sugar, depending on the sweetness of the fruit

½ cup [120 ml] filtered or spring water

Aromatics, such as cinnamon, cloves, cardamon, or knob of ginger (optional; sometimes I keep it simple and omit the aromatics)

Weigh the fruit. Measure out a quarter of the weight of the fruit in sugar. In a large pot, mix the fruit and sugar until well combined. Allow this mixture to sit for 1 hour to macerate.

Measure out a quarter of the fruit weight in water. Add the water and any aromatics (if using) to the pot with the fruit and sugar. Bring up to a simmer and reduce until the consistency is thick but spreadable, about 30 minutes. If making a molasses, reduce slightly longer until the consistency is very thick, about another 15 minutes. Jam or molasses keeps for 1 month in the refrigerator.

Fruit Tonic Master Recipe

MAKES 2½ CUPS [600 ML]

2 cups [about 300 g] fruit, such as Concord grapes (my favorite), cranberries, peaches, or pineapple, roughly chopped if large

1 to 2 Tbsp chopped fresh herbs, such as lemon verbena, sage, or rosemary, or whole spices, such as cardamom pods, cinnamon stick, star anise, or aniseed (optional)

2 Tbsp cane sugar, maple syrup, honey, or another natural sweetener

2 Tbsp cider vinegar or lemon juice

2 cups [480 ml] filtered water

Add the fruit, herbs and spices (if using), and sugar to a 3 cup [720 ml] sterile glass container. Mash well with a pestle or with your hands. Cover and let it sit overnight. The next day, add the vinegar and mix well. Boil the filtered water and pour over the mixture. Cover and leave it out overnight. The following day, strain the liquid into a sterile bottle or jar and discard the solids. Store in a lidded container in the refrigerator for 1 month.

Uses
Mix it with sparkling water for a fizzy treat any time of day or add to hot water for a tea. It's also great as a topping for a yogurt or fruit bowl, or as a base for a vinaigrette dressing with a little oil, salt, and an extra splash of acid.

Dish
Fruit Bowl (page 126)

Apricot Saffron Compote

MAKES 2 CUPS [600 G]

2 Tbsp cane sugar

1½ cups [360 ml] plus 1 Tbsp water

2 Tbsp apple cider vinegar

20 strands saffron

1 cup [150 g] dried apricots

ADD-INS (OPTIONAL):

Hard spice, such as cinnamon stick, star anise, or cardamom pods

Zest and juice of a small orange

½ tsp rose or orange blossom water

A few drops of vanilla extract

When I use granulated cane sugar for compotes, I find that the flavor lacks the dimension that maple syrup or honey have. So, I like to caramelize the sugar a bit to give it more edge.

Add the sugar and 1 Tbsp of the water to a small pot over medium-high heat. Do not stir. Keep an eye on the sugar; once it turns amber in color, carefully add the vinegar first and then the remaining 1½ cups [360 ml] water. Make sure to have the vinegar and water at the ready, because the sugar can burn quickly. Add the saffron and any optional add-ins and bring the mixture to a boil. Once boiling, add in the dried apricots. Turn the heat to low, cover, and simmer for 5 minutes. After 5 minutes, stir, re-cover, and cook for an additional 10 minutes. After 10 minutes, turn off the heat and bring down to room temperature without uncovering. This compote keeps in a lidded container in the refrigerator for 1 week.

Uses
Deep in the winter when the markets are low on fruit, I'll eat compotes right out of the jar. They're great on yogurt, ice cream, or pavlovas. Try using the same ratio of dried prunes, figs, or cherries for a different take.

Dishes
Couscous Porridge with Rhubarb and Apricot Saffron Compote (page 130)

Plum Molasses

MAKES 2 CUPS [640 G]

4 cups [about 600 g] pitted and chopped plums

¾ cup [150 g] cane sugar

1 cinnamon stick

1 cup [240 ml] water

Add the plums, sugar, and cinnamon stick to a medium pot, mix well, and let sit for 1 hour to macerate. After an hour of maceration, add the water and bring the mixture to a simmer over medium heat, then decrease the heat to low. Simmer for 15 minutes, stirring occasionally. Remove the cinnamon stick and strain the plum mixture through a fine-mesh sieve or purée in a blender until smooth. Transfer to a sterile jar and store in the refrigerator for 2 months.

Uses
Swirl this molasses into yogurt or smoothies, or add it to savory sauces for a tart-sweet dimension.

Dish
Noodle Bowl with Carrots and Fresh Herbs (page 211)

Cranberry-Hibiscus Molasses

MAKES 1 CUP [320 G]

1 lb [455 g] fresh or frozen cranberries

1 cup [240 ml] filtered water

½ cup [100 g] cane sugar

¼ cup [7 g] dried whole hibiscus flowers (see Note)

Add the cranberries, water, sugar, and hibiscus to a large pot and slowly bring to a simmer over low heat. Simmer for 5 minutes. Strain through a fine-mesh sieve. Transfer to a sterile jar and store in the refrigerator for 2 months.

NOTE: If you do not have whole hibiscus flowers, you can add loose hibiscus tea from a tea bag or sachet.

Uses
I like to pair thick, rich fruit molasses with earthier flavors, and this is great added to a dressing for a beet or chicory salad.

Dishes
Sweet Oat and Rice Porridge (page 129)

Noodle Bowl with Carrots and Fresh Herbs (page 211)

Guava Jam or Paste

MAKES ½ CUP [120 G] JAM OR ¼ CUP [60 G] PASTE

2 lb [910 g] peeled guava or quince, sliced in half (see Note)

1 cinnamon stick (optional)

3 cups [720 ml] filtered or spring water

¼ cup [50 g] cane sugar

To make the jam: Peel and halve the guava. Scoop out the seeds. In a medium pot, add the guava seeds, cinnamon stick (if using), and water. Simmer, covered, over low heat for 15 minutes. Meanwhile, cut the peeled guava into 1 in [2.5 cm] pieces. Once the fruit around the seeds has disintegrated, strain, keeping the water, now tinted amber, and add it back to the pot, discarding the seeds and cinnamon stick. Add the cut guava fruit and sugar and simmer for 1 hour until it breaks down and has the consistency of smooth applesauce. Transfer to a clean jar. This jam keeps for 2 weeks in the refrigerator.

To make the paste: Continue stirring so that the jam does not stick to the bottom of the pot. Cook until it's dark red and dense, about 40 minutes more. Transfer to a slightly oiled pan lined with parchment paper. Set for 8 hours in the refrigerator. Slice and serve with cheese.

NOTE: Quince is similar in texture and flavor to guava, and is often more readily available, so it is a good substitute if you are unable to source fresh guava.

Uses

The jam is great to dollop on a yogurt or fruit bowl with grated fresh ginger. Pour the paste into a mold to create an interesting addition to a simple and satisfying last course of cheese along with a slightly chilled red wine.

Dish

Cheese Biscuits with Guava Jam (page 142)

Pear and Meyer Lemon Jam

MAKES 2 CUPS [350 G]

3 or 4 pears [600 g], peeled, cored, and cut into cubes

2 Meyer lemons [200 g], sliced thinly with a mandoline

¾ cup [180 g] maple syrup or other natural sweetener

3 whole dried hibiscus flowers (optional, see Note)

Add the pears, lemons, maple syrup, and hibiscus (if using) to a medium pot, mix well, and let sit for 1 hour to macerate. After an hour of maceration, bring the mixture up to a simmer over medium heat, then decrease the heat to low. Stir occasionally. After 45 minutes, remove the hibiscus flowers and mash the mixture with a potato masher or large pestle until the consistency resembles applesauce. Continue cooking over low heat for another 15 minutes, stirring every couple of minutes, to let the flavors meld a bit more before pulling it off to cool. Transfer to a clean jar. This jam keeps for 2 weeks in the refrigerator.

NOTE: If you do not have whole hibiscus flowers, you can add loose hibiscus tea from a tea bag or sachet.

Uses

This is great to dollop on a yogurt or fruit bowl or slathered over a buttery piece of toast.

Dish

Fruit Bowl (page 126)

FINISHINGS

Like a special outfit without jewelry, your mise en place is not complete without the finishes. Ideally, these finishes add another dimension of flavor and health properties along with a visual element to the dish. Every cuisine has their own seed, nut, and powder finishings: Gomasio, the Japanese sesame salt condiment, has always played a part in macrobiotic philosophy, and dukkah from Egypt is a traditional condiment that elevates many dishes. Having a nice assortment of finishings on hand is also fantastic for spontaneous cooking. Melon with a salt mix and olive oil or a dusting of Fruit Powder (page 115) becomes a very special thing. These flourishes can also provide protein or incorporate superfood adaptogens or herbal powders into your daily life. Most of all, they make cooking fun. It's a chance to be creative and connect with your cravings even if you only have time to sprinkle on a bit of something special.

SEED AND NUT MIXES

I always have some seed or nut mixes on hand because it's easy to use them to dress up everyday staples such as salad, steamed vegetables, or rice. In many ways, these little mixes are a distinct topping that I consider a secret weapon in my cooking arsenal—they are what help set my creations apart. If I buy edible flowers or herbs for a salad and realize I will not use them all, I dry them. Once they are dry, I mix them with other sundries to make beautiful, bright, herby seed and nut mixes, gomasios, or seasoned salt mixes. Be aware that seeds and nuts go rancid quickly, so always store them away from your stove. Place them instead in a cooler area of your kitchen or, if you won't be using them daily, in your refrigerator.

Gomasio
Master Recipe

YIELD VARIES

18 parts white or black sesame seeds to 1 part sea salt

In a dry skillet over medium heat, toast the seeds while stirring constantly until aromatic and beginning to pop, 2 to 3 minutes. Add the seeds and salt to a mortar and pound with the pestle until most of the seeds have been slightly nicked. If using a food processor, be aware that leaving the processor going too long can cause your seeds to become paste. I advise you to pulse three times and check, repeating until the consistency is that of coarse sand. This will keep in a lidded container for 1 month at room temperature or 3 months in the refrigerator.

Roasted Nut
Master Recipe

Oil-roasting nuts allows them to pick up seasonings for flavor building. Roasting in the oven is ideal if you're making enough to warrant preheating an oven, but if not, consider using a toaster oven instead. Roasting on the stove top requires constant attention and tossing, so I rarely make my nuts that way. I usually oven-roast a big batch and commit to using them up within the week.

MAKES 1 CUP [140 G]

1 cup [140 g] whole nuts, such as almonds, pecans, walnuts, or cashews

1 tsp neutral oil, such as sunflower, grapeseed, safflower, or rice bran

¼ tsp salt

Pinch chili powder

Additional seasonings, such as cumin for savory applications or cardamom for sweet applications (optional)

Preheat the oven to 400°F [200°C] or the toaster oven to high. Line a baking sheet with parchment paper.

In a bowl, add the nuts and drizzle with the oil. Toss to evenly coat. Sprinkle with the salt, chili powder, and any other seasonings (if using) and toss to coat. Spread on the prepared baking sheet and roast for approximately 7 minutes in the oven or 5 minutes in the toaster oven.

For a special treat, via Alice Waters, slow-roast nuts dressed in olive oil, loads of fresh sage, and salt at 275°F [140°C] for 35 minutes.

This will keep in a lidded container for 1 month at room temperature or 3 months in the refrigerator.

Sesame, Cranberry Seed, and Safflower Gomasio

MAKES ABOUT ¾ CUP [120 G]

½ cup [70 g] white sesame seeds

¼ cup [25 g] cranberry seeds

1 Tbsp sea salt

2 Tbsp dried safflower blossoms or other dried edible flower

2 Tbsp cranberry powder

Add the sesame seeds, cranberry seeds, and salt to a mortar and pound with the pestle until most of the sesame seeds have been nicked. Transfer the seed mixture to a bowl and stir in the safflower and cranberry powder. This will keep in a lidded container for 1 month at room temperature or 3 months in the refrigerator. The longer this sits, the tangier it gets.

Uses
This gomasio is versatile and great for both sweet and savory dishes. Sprinkle on cold or warm cereal, buttered honey toast, or savory dishes such as crudos, crudités, salads, and rice.

Dish
Sweet or Savory Oat and Rice Porridge
(page 129)

Summer Gomasio

MAKES ½ CUP [70 G]

8 parsley sprigs

8 flowering herb sprigs, such as mint, thyme, or basil (see Note)

¼ cup [1.5 g] edible flowers

½ cup [70 g] toasted sesame seeds

2 tsp sea salt

Gently wash the parsley, herbs, and flowers, then lay them on a flat basket or rack to dry for a week (alternatively, use a dehydrator over-night). With your fingers, crumble the herbs into a mortar. Discard any stems and reserve the flower heads. Add the sesame seeds and salt and pound with the pestle until most of the sesame seeds have been nicked. Add the flower heads and pound a couple of times to incorporate. This mix will keep in a lidded container for 1 month at room temperature or 3 months in the refrigerator.

NOTE: In late summer when everything is peaking at the market or in your gardens, grab up all the flowering herbs and edible flowers you can and dry them for later use. Flowering herbs have an extra boost of flavor, making them ideal for drying and using in this appli-cation. If none are available, dried herbs with-out the blossoms will do fine.

Uses
Use this mix as you would a standard finishing salt for salads, dips, soups, steamed vegetables, fish, and more.

Dishes
Dressed Rice with Shiso and Summer Gomasio
(page 228)

Noodle Bowl with Carrots and Fresh Herbs
(page 211)

Sweet or Savory Oat and Rice Porridge
(page 129)

Seaweed Gomasio

MAKES ½ CUP [70 G]

½ cup [70 g] toasted black sesame seeds

2 Tbsp salt

2 Tbsp aonori seaweed or chopped nori

Combine the sesame seeds, salt, and seaweed in a food processor and pulse until most of the sesame seeds are nicked, but be careful not to overprocess it to a powder. This keeps for 2 to 3 weeks at room temperature or 3 months in the refrigerator.

Uses
Use this as a topping for rice, eggs, avocado, salads, soups, fish, and beyond.

Dish
Chicories and Seaweeds (page 187)

Toasted Cacao Nib, Buckwheat, and Sesame Mix

MAKES ¾ CUP [85 G]

¼ cup [60 ml] neutral oil, such as sunflower, grapeseed, safflower, or rice bran

½ cup [180 g] buckwheat groats

Salt

Chili powder

¼ cup [30 g] cacao nibs

2 Tbsp black sesame seeds

Heat the oil in a pan over medium heat until hot. Add the buckwheat and move the grains around until they begin to pop and toast. With a slotted spoon, transfer the buckwheat to paper towels to drain. Sprinkle a pinch of salt and chili powder over them while they are still hot. Add the cacao nibs to the pan with the residual oil and toast for a couple of minutes, remove, drain, and salt as you did the buckwheat. The pan should have a minimal amount of residual oil by this time—if not, remove any excess with a paper towel. Add the sesame seeds and toast until fragrant. Transfer to a mortar with a pinch of salt and pound with the pestle until each seed is nicked. Mix the buckwheat, cacao nibs, and seeds together. This mix keeps in a lidded container for 2 weeks at room temperature or 3 months in the refrigerator.

Uses
Cacao is rich in antioxidants; I find myself wanting to add it to everything at times. Using it in savory dishes brings out a nuttiness and a complexity of flavor that I really enjoy. This mix also has an amazing crunch quality from both the cacao nibs and the toasted buckwheat, so you can enjoy it on steamed verdant spring vegetables or roasted hearty winter roots and squashes or even sprinkle a bit on top of granola.

Dish
Salt-Baked Vegetables with Cacao Seed Mix (page 209)

Turmeric-Chili Almonds

MAKES 1 CUP [100 G]

1 cup [100 g] sliced almonds

½ tsp kosher salt

¼ tsp ground turmeric

Small pinch chili powder

2 Tbsp desiccated coconut or dried coconut flakes (optional)

1 Tbsp sesame seeds (optional)

Preheat the oven to 400°F [200°C]. Line a baking sheet with parchment paper.

In a bowl, toss the almonds, salt, turmeric, and chili powder together and spread them out on the prepared baking sheet. Roast for 5 minutes, add the coconut and sesame seeds (if using), give them a flip with a metal spatula, and roast for another 2 to 3 minutes. This mix keeps in a lidded container for 2 weeks at room temperature or 3 months in the refrigerator.

Uses
Pile these onto a crunchy salad, such as one with fennel and Parmesan cheese. Or add large raw coconut shavings and sesame to the mix to give it a summer spin for a tart green mango salad.

Dish
Turmeric Lentil Rice with Mustard and Cumin Seeds (page 233)

Everything Dukkah Mix

MAKES 1¼ CUPS [135 G]

1 cup [100 g] salted, roasted nuts (see page 105), coarsely chopped

¼ cup [30 g] dry-roasted seeds, such as sesame, hemp, cranberry, poppy, or nigella, or puffed buckwheat groats

1 Tbsp Spice Mix Master Recipe (page 117)

Mix all the ingredients together. This mix will keep in a lidded container for 2 weeks at room temperature or 3 months in the refrigerator.

Uses
Use as a topping for dips, soups, salads, roasted vegetables, and dressed rice dishes.

Dishes
Turmeric Lentil Rice with Mustard and Cumin Seeds (page 233)

Flatbread with Spiced Oil and Everything Dukkah Mix (page 138)

POWER POWDERS

I love to dust nutritional powders on my finished dishes to add color and an extra boost of nutrients. But the powders that are most commonly found in the market, such as mushroom adaptogen powder, moringa, and collagen, aren't very pleasant on their own. So I started making my own by mixing these powders with other, tastier ones like lemon powder and nutritional yeast to balance the flavors. It's a sneaky way to eat healthy without making it obvious, while also giving dishes big flavor.

Power Powder Master Recipe

YIELD VARIES

2 parts nutritional yeast

1 part lemon powder, homemade (see Note) or store-bought

1 part savory herb, vegetable, or superfood powder (see Note)

In a bowl, mix the nutritional yeast, lemon powder, and savory powder together and taste. If the flavor isn't coming through enough, add more of the savory powder until it's to your liking. Store in a lidded container at room temperature for 6 months.

NOTE: Herb and vegetable powders can be purchased or made at home by dehydrating or drying herbs, citrus peel, mushrooms, or vegetables and grinding them to a powder in a spice grinder.

Spirulina-Lemon Powder a.k.a. Magic Powder

MAKES ½ CUP [45 G]

¼ cup [20 g] nutritional yeast

2 Tbsp spirulina

2 Tbsp lemon powder, homemade (see Note, left) or store-bought

Using a delicate hand, mix the nutritional yeast, spirulina, and lemon powder together in a bowl. Store in a lidded container at room temperature for 6 months.

Uses
This powder loves a hearty rich green salad like kale and watercress with a tangy-sweet dressing.

Dish
Chicories and Seaweeds (page 187)

Super-Powered Powder

MAKES ½ CUP [45 G]

¼ cup [20 g] nutritional yeast

2 Tbsp reishi, chaga, or lion's mane powder

2 Tbsp lemon powder, homemade (see Note, page 111) or store-bought

1 tsp ground turmeric

¼ tsp ground black pepper

In a bowl, whisk together the nutritional yeast, reishi powder, lemon powder, turmeric, and pepper. Store in a lidded container at room temperature for 6 months.

Uses
This powder is a boost of umami and nutrients, and popcorn found its match with this one. I also like to add this to fresh corn polenta or rice porridge with an egg, and it works well on most salads, especially ones with bitter greens.

Dishes
Shaved Mushroom, Dandelion, and Petal Salad (page 197)

Quick Adaptogenic Moka Pot Sipping Broth (page 150)

Black Pepper Umami Powder

MAKES ¼ CUP [20 G]

¼ cup [30 g] fermented black beans

1 Tbsp coarsely ground black peppercorns

1 tsp adaptogenic mushroom powder

Add the black beans to a food processor and pulse until finely minced. Transfer to a medium bowl, add the peppercorns and mushroom powder, and mix thoroughly. The peppercorns should help break down any lumps from the black beans. Store in a lidded container at room temperature for 6 months.

Uses
This is a great sprinkle for a crushed cucumber salad or for finishing sautéed green vegetables.

Dishes
Salt and Pepper Seafood Fry (page 251)

Steamed Porgy with Fresh Ginger and Black Pepper Umami Powder (page 255)

Fruit Powder

MAKES ½ CUP [42 G]

¼ cup [25 g] fruit powder (see Note)

1½ Tbsp lemon powder, homemade (see Note, page 111) or store-bought

1½ Tbsp organic superfine cane sugar (optional)

Mix the fruit and lemon powder together in a bowl. Some fruit powders are sufficiently sweet, so taste yours before you incorporate the sugar to make sure it needs it. Store in a lidded container at room temperature for 6 months.

NOTE: Store-bought dehydrated fruit powders are becoming more and more available, but you can make your own by dehydrating any favorite or excess fruit you have, then grinding it in a spice grinder. I like to sift the powder before using so it's fine.

Uses
I started using fruit powders to lend beauty to a plate and quickly figured out that some fruits need to be heightened with just a touch of tartness, which is why I like to kick mine up with lemon powder. Dust onto yogurt, ice cream, porridge, cold cereals and granola, pavlovas, crêpes, or cakes.

Dishes
Puffed Granola with Fruit Powder (page 132)

Fruit Bowl (page 126)

FINISHING OILS

High-quality oils, such as extra-virgin olive oil and sesame oil, are not meant to be cooked with, but are instead used to add wonderful finishing to a dish. Some people would go as far as to say that plain extra-virgin olive oil is the best sauce. It elevates the dish, finishes it off, and gives it a sauciness and richness. Oils can be very volatile, and they can go bad quickly. Ideally, you want to use a bottle of oil within a month of opening it, especially for high-quality oils. Be sure to store them away from heat to preserve them. For some dishes, like pastas and fish, I love adding a finishing oil. It's also good for finishing dips like hummus, which sings with a spiced oil, or a yogurt dip that's punched up with herb oil. Sometimes I like adding a bit of finishing oil to saucy dishes, such as beans, stews, and soups, because I find it makes them exceptionally velvety.

Spiced Finishing Oil Master Recipe

MAKES 1¼ CUPS [250 ML]

3 Tbsp Spice Mix Master Recipe (right) or other blend of spices (see Note)

1 cup [240 ml] neutral oil, such as sunflower, grapeseed, safflower, or rice bran

Add the spices to a heatproof bowl. In a small pot over medium-high heat, warm the oil until it reaches a temperature of 375°F [190°C]. Carefully pour the hot oil over the spices. Let cool. Store in a lidded container at room temperature for 2 weeks.

NOTE: Use whatever spices you like and have on hand, but the Spice Mix Master Recipe (right), red pepper flakes, or cracked coriander seed are some great options.

Spice Mix Master Recipe

YIELD VARIES

1 part cayenne pepper

2 parts ground or whole mustard seeds

2 parts ground or whole fennel seeds

3 parts ground or whole cumin seeds

3 parts ground or whole coriander seeds

If using ground spices, mix them together and warm in a dry skillet before use. If using whole seeds, toast each variety of seed separately in a dry skillet and pulse in a spice grinder or pound with a mortar and pestle until it becomes a powder. Store in a jar at room temperature for 1 year.

Crispy Honey Chili Oil

MAKES 4 CUPS [960 ML]

2 cups [70 g] dried whole chiles, such as Kashmiri, árbol, Japones, Guerrero, ancho, or a mix (see Note)

¼ cup [35 g] roasted peanuts, soy nuts, or sesame seeds (see page 105)

2 Tbsp mushroom powder or adaptogen mushroom powder blend

¼ cup [30 g] fermented black beans, finely chopped

2 Tbsp sugar

1 Tbsp ground black pepper

1 tsp salt

3 cardamom pods

2 cups [480 ml] neutral oil, such as sunflower, grapeseed, safflower, or rice bran

1 cup [50 g] thinly sliced shallots (see Note)

¼ cup [35 g] thinly sliced garlic (see Note)

½ cup [170 g] honey

½ cup [120 ml] sesame oil

Place a wire rack over a baking sheet. Using gloves, remove the stems from the chiles with scissors and cut the chiles lengthwise. Place the chiles on the rack facedown. Shake the rack to sift out most of the seeds. Transfer just the chiles to a blender or spice grinder, working in batches, and process them to resemble commercial red pepper flakes.

In a large heatproof bowl, mix together the peanuts, mushroom powder, fermented black beans, sugar, pepper, salt, and cardamom. Mix in the blended pepper flakes and set aside.

Place a fine-mesh metal sieve over a heatproof bowl and set aside. Add the neutral oil and shallots to a small pot over medium-low heat and allow them to come up in temperature for about 20 minutes, stirring occasionally to prevent sticking, until the shallots are golden brown.

Once the shallots are done, pour the oil through the sieve and set the strained shallots aside in a small bowl. Allow the oil to cool. Wipe the pot clean and transfer the oil back to the pot. Repeat the same process with the sliced garlic.

Wipe the pot of any residual garlic. Transfer the oil back to the pot and warm over medium heat until it reaches 375°F [190°C]. Carefully pour the oil over the reserved chile and spice mixture; it will bubble up for a second or two. Add the honey and mix well. Allow this mixture to cool completely before adding the sesame oil and the fried shallots and garlic; this will ensure they stay crispy. Transfer to a glass jar and store at room temperature away from heat for 2 months.

NOTE: Alternatively, you can use ½ cup [40 g] high-quality red pepper flakes. When slicing shallots and garlic, use a mandoline; slices must be uniform to ensure even goldenness throughout.

Uses
This condiment was essentially inspired by salsa macha, the Mexican chile condiment with peanuts, as well as Chinese chili crisp. This is literally a topping for all—I've even seen it on ice cream.

Dishes
Smoked Fish and Squash Blossom Pancake with Crispy Honey Chili Oil (page 173)

Turkish Eggs with Crispy Honey Chili Oil (page 159)

Kombu Oil

MAKES 2 CUPS [480 ML]

1 sheet [20 grams] kombu

A generous handful [150 g] dark leafy greens such as kale, collard, or spinach

2 cups [480 ml] neutral oil, such as grapeseed

Place a fine-mesh sieve over a large metal bowl.

Place a cast-iron skillet or other heavy-bottom pan over medium-high heat. When very hot, toast the kombu until it turns from green to brown. Remove from the pan from the heat.

In a high-powered blender, add the toasted kombu, greens, and oil. Blend on high speed until smooth, about 30 seconds. Add the mixture to the still-warm pan and stir until just warmed through.

Pour the mixture into the sieve, allowing the green oil to strain into the bowl, from 2 to 6 hours. Discard the pulp (or use, see Note) and store the oil at room temperature in a lidded container for up to 1 week.

NOTE: If using beet greens or Swiss chard, remove the red stems to maintain a bright green color in the oil. The pulp remaining in the strainer can be used in sauces or as a soup base or finisher.

Vanilla Oil

MAKES 2 CUPS [480 ML]

2 cups [480 ml] extra-virgin olive oil

½ vanilla pod, halved lengthwise

In a glass jar or bottle, add the oil and vanilla pod and let steep for 1 or 2 days before using. Store in a lidded container at room temperature for up to 1 week.

Uses
Drizzle over thinly sliced tomato and flaky sea salt or add a little over a gratin dish. You can also use in baking when a recipe calls for oil.

Dish
Savory Lemon Focaccia (page 140)

DISHES

A well-rounded dish is easily created from a well-stocked pantry; the mixing and matching options are endless. Say you have a yogurt sauce and ripe tomatoes ready to use. Think: "What do I have in my pantry? What sauce can I make? What can I use to finish it? What does my body need and want today?" As you begin cooking, taste everything as you go. Make sure that the acidity is good, that the salt is right, and that it is juicy and saucy. By applying the lessons and elements from the previous section, you can have the creative freedom and trust to develop dishes on your own.

I rarely make the same recipe twice—I'm always changing it up or tweaking it to make it better. And I rarely make a recipe that I may find in a cookbook exactly how it's written (I know this is a bold statement to make in a cookbook). Instead, I use it as inspiration and sub in what I have, including leftovers, while also being mindful of what will go bad soon. One day of cooking always bleeds into the next. You want to make a dish that's nourishing while, at the same time, considering its components: the star, or main component; the flavor, such as the sauce; and the jewel, or garnish.

What follows is a collage of dishes inspired by those I've created throughout my career, as well as recipes and techniques I've picked up from family and friends. This section is arranged to follow the cycle of a day, from morning to evening, and are all composed of the pantry elements from part 1 (page 31). Once you start to play around with these elements, you will see how easy it is to begin to trust your instincts to create your own tasty, nourishing dishes.

FRUITS AND CEREALS

For me, mornings are about taking a moment to meditate and connect before exercising or stepping into the work hustle. We all have special ways of breaking our fast, and that can change daily. Sometimes our bodies crave small meals that gently glide us back into waking hours, and other times we hunger to eat heartier meals, to build energy to carry us through a busy morning.

As always, pay attention to what's in season as you cook. There's a luxury to taking time to start your day with a plate of local peak fruit in the summer, toast with smashed peas and a saucy drizzle in the spring, or warm porridges with poached fruit in cooler months. The recipes in this section are easily adaptable to include fruits and vegetables from the season you're in. But don't forget to consider your pantry—frozen summer berries and fruits can be a special treat to carry you through the winter months.

ANATOMY

of a Fruit Bowl

I like to start the day with something fresh, and when I want something a little sweet, I always turn to a fruit bowl. It's beautiful and simple, clean and adaptable, and I take pleasure in the act of composing the dish: cutting the fruit, arranging it on a plate, topping and swirling in a variety of ingredients for that perfect bite. Unlike a traditional smoothie or yogurt bowl, the fruit, rather than the base, is the star of the dish. Although it's minimal effort, it's an intentional act, a peaceful start to the day. Take pleasure from creating your own combinations from some of my suggestions below.

To prepare, add your base to a bowl or plate. Arrange your fruits on top of the base. Drizzle, sprinkle, or dollop on toppings and dressing, and serve.

Base

Yogurt

Porridge

Smoothie

Milk

Fruits

SPRING: Rhubarb, Asian pear

SUMMER: Stone fruit, berries, grapes

FALL: Pears, cranberries, persimmons, chopped or grated apples dressed in lemon juice, pomegranate, quince, kiwi

WINTER: Citrus, dates and other whole dried fruits, passion fruit

Toppings

Fresh ginger, grated on a Microplane

Jams, marmalades, and fruit molasses (page 98)

Fruit powders (page 115)

Seeds and nuts, either whole or as a mix (page 105)

Dressing

Fruit tonics (page 99)

Honey

Maple syrup

Inspirational Flavor Combos

Fruit salad with Fruit Powder (page 115)

Tahini Yogurt (page 36) with Apricot Saffron Compote (page 99)

Guava Jam (page 101) with fresh grated ginger and yogurt

Pear and Meyer Lemon Jam (page 101) with ripe persimmon and yogurt

SWEET OR SAVORY OAT AND RICE PORRIDGE

Makes 1 or 2 servings

My love of porridge comes from working and living in a Zen center in my early twenties. It was served most mornings—rice, oats, or five-grain cereal mix that I still search for everywhere, topped with reconstituted dried apricots and prunes that were so plump and flavorful it was often hard to determine whether they were in fact dried. This is a wonderfully versatile dish: It can be savory or sweet, and is a great way to use leftover rice.

2 cups [480 ml] filtered or spring water
2 Tbsp rice flour
¼ cup [30 g] cooked grains, such as rice or quinoa
2 Tbsp old-fashioned oats

In a small pot, combine the water and rice flour and whisk well. Add the cooked grains and oats. Cover and cook over low heat for 20 minutes, stirring occasionally to prevent it from sticking. Transfer the porridge to one or two bowls and serve.

For a savory porridge:
Swirl in 1 Tbsp Miso Butter (page 70) or Green Tahini (page 54) and top with ¼ green onion, thinly sliced, and a pinch of sesame seeds or Summer Gomasio (page 106).

For a sweet porridge:
Swirl with 1 to 2 Tbsp Cranberry-Hibiscus Molasses (page 100) or one of the compotes from the Compote Master Recipe (page 98), then top with a sprinkle of Sesame, Cranberry Seed, and Safflower Gomasio (page 106).

COUSCOUS PORRIDGE WITH RHUBARB AND APRICOT SAFFRON COMPOTE

Serves 2 to 4

Although I know it's not very common to see couscous used as a porridge base, I love it because of the texture and quick preparation time. Plus, the couscous has a natural sweetness that works really well paired with a sweet compote or with warm almond milk poured over. It's an unusual and delicately flavored way to start the day.

1¼ cups [300 ml] filtered water, plus more as needed
¼ cup [55 g] pearl couscous
¼ cup [40 g] couscous
Milk (optional)
2 cups [600 g] Apricot Saffron Compote (page 99)
2 rhubarb stalks, cut into 3 in [7.5 cm] pieces

In a small pot, add the water and pearl couscous. Bring up to a simmer over medium-low heat, stir, decrease the heat to low, cover, and cook for 12 minutes. Stir in the regular couscous. Cover and remove from the heat. Let sit for 5 minutes, then fluff with a fork. Add water or milk if the couscous is too thick.

In a pot, warm the compote to a simmer, add the rhubarb, remove from the heat, cover, and let sit for 5 minutes until the rhubarb is tender.

Portion the couscous out into bowls, top each with about a ½ cup [150 g] of the compote, and serve.

PUFFED GRANOLA WITH FRUIT POWDER

Makes 8 servings

I love the idea of eating granola, but sometimes the somewhat raw whole grains are hard for me to digest. Instead, I buy puffed grains, which are already cooked. Plus, they're so nostalgic—this recipe, in particular, reminds me of the grown-up version of Honey Smacks cereal.

1 cup [30 g] puffed large grains, such as kamut or wheat
½ cup [10 g] puffed small grains, such as amaranth or millet
¼ cup [35 g] sunflower seeds
½ tsp salt
½ tsp ground cinnamon
¼ tsp ground ginger
¼ tsp ground black pepper
¼ tsp ground allspice
¼ cup [50 g] organic cane sugar
¼ cup [85 g] honey
2 Tbsp glucose or organic corn syrup
¼ tsp baking soda
2 Tbsp seeds, such as sesame, hemp, poppy, or cranberry
¼ cup [35 g] sliced dates or other dried fruit (optional)

Preheat the oven to 325°F [170°C]. Line a baking sheet with parchment paper.

In a large heatproof bowl, add the puffed grains, sunflower seeds, salt, cinnamon, ginger, pepper, and allspice and mix well.

In a small saucepan, add the sugar, honey, and glucose. Bring to a boil until it reaches 250°F [120°C]. Remove from the heat. Add the baking soda, mixing immediately until it bubbles up. Quickly pour the syrup over the grains and spice mixture, mixing together until all the grains are coated. Working fast is key, as the syrup hardens and you'll want to have covered as much of the grains as possible before it does.

Quickly spread out the coated grains onto the prepared baking sheet. Bake for 10 minutes. Remove from the oven and immediately sprinkle with the sesame seeds while the grains are still tacky. Once cool, mix in the dried fruit (if using).

Store in a lidded container at room temperature for about a month (do not store in the refrigerator, as the moisture from the condensation will make the puffed grains soggy). Enjoy with milk as a cereal, with yogurt as a granola, or by the handful as a snack.

BAKED

I am a sweet-treat-in-the-middle-of-the-day-with-tea type of person, and the recipes in this section reflect that. For a lot of my career, I considered myself too peppy to be on bakers' time, but COVID-19 allowed me to bring more calm and mindfulness to my baking practice.

I dislike consuming refined sugar, as I find it heavy on the palate and very bad for your body, so I take it upon myself to bake my own cakes, cookies, and pies so I can control the sweetness. Usually when I bake using a recipe I didn't develop, I swap the white sugar for natural sweeteners, such as granulated cane sugar, honey, or maple syrup, cut the sugar by a quarter, and increase the salt by a pinch or two more. I find that the sweetness becomes much more balanced, and I can taste the other elements better.

I also try to limit my intake of refined commercial bleached wheat flour, as it's often factory farmed, overprocessed, and chemically engineered. Ideally, I purchase flour that's grown and milled locally, but store-bought organic, unbleached flour is good. If you're in a pinch and can't find organic, unbleached flour will work.

I prefer to do my baking in the morning when everything feels slow and easy, with the added bonus that it gives my treats time to rest and cool before my afternoon break.

GO-TO DOUGH

If I'm not purchasing my bread from a reliable baker I know to use quality flour, then I'm going to bake my own. I developed this go-to dough as a versatile, reliable, always-has-the-same-results recipe that can be used as a base for everything from focaccia to pizza to flatbread.

This back-pocket recipe is intended to help you get the hang of baking with yeast and sourdough starter. It'll help you nail simple bread every single time, hopefully giving you the confidence to move into more complicated bread recipes as your baking practice grows.

I have developed a preference for making smaller portions of baked goods because (a) I believe most baked items are best the same day they're baked and (b) to conserve energy; why heat a large oven when a toaster uses a fraction of the energy? This recipe is toaster-oven size, so double the recipe for a regular oven-size baking sheet.

3 tsp yeast or ¼ cup [50 g] sourdough starter
(see Note)

½ cup [120 ml] filtered water, warm

¼ cup [60 g] plain yogurt

1 tsp honey or other natural sweetener

1½ cups [210 g] all-purpose flour, plus more
as needed

2 Tbsp olive oil

1 tsp salt

In a medium bowl, mix the yeast or sourdough
starter with the water, yogurt, and honey. Let sit
for 5 minutes or until you see some bubbly activity
(always check the date of your yeast, as it won't
work if it's out of date). Add the flour, oil, and salt
and mix until combined.

Transfer to an oiled container with a lid and refrigerate overnight and up to 72 hours, as the dough's
flavor matures with time. If you're using dough
that's been refrigerated, it will need to come to
room temperature before proofing, so let it rest on
the counter for up to 2 hours before adding to a
bowl and allowing to rise. But if you're baking this
at the last minute and don't have the time to wait
overnight, flour a clean surface and knead the
dough for 10 minutes, adding up to ¼ cup [30 g]
of additional flour if the dough is too sticky. You
should be able to knead it without it sticking to
your hands. Add the dough to a large bowl, cover
it with a tea towel or plate, and allow it to rest
and double in size in a warm place, such as an
unheated oven with the oven light on for 1 hour.

To make focaccia: Preheat the oven to 400°F
[200°C]. Line a 6 by 9 in [15 by 23 cm] pan with
parchment and grease the parchment. Spread
the dough in the pan and let proof on the counter
for 1 hour if the dough is cold or 30 minutes if the
dough is warm, until it doubles in size again. With
your fingers, make dimples throughout the surface
of the dough, then drizzle with olive oil and add
any toppings. Bake until golden brown, about
20 minutes.

To make flatbreads: Divide the dough into
8 (approximately 50 g) pieces. Roll into balls,
place on parchment paper, a plate, or directly on
the clean counter, and cover with a clean dish
towel. Let them proof for 30 minutes if the dough
is cold, or 15 to 20 minutes if the dough is warm.
Heat a cast-iron or grill pan over medium-high
heat. On a floured or oiled surface, flatten and

stretch each ball with your hands or a rolling pin
into ⅛ in [3 mm] thick, 4 or 5 in [10 or 12.5 cm]
rounds. If you'd like, you can add a bit of neutral
oil to the skillet and immediately pop your rolled
dough onto it (you can also make them in a dry,
unoiled skillet or on a grill over a fire). Cook until
the bottom is toasty, 1 to 2 minutes, flip, and cook
for an additional 1 to 2 minutes until both sides are
browned. Remove from the skillet, add any toppings you'd like (see Toppings), and serve warm.

NOTE: During COVID-19, the sourdough trend
hit, and everyone was scrambling to get some
mother (the loving term used to refer to sourdough starter). But after some experimenting, I
realized you can very easily make a quick mother
using store-bought yeast. And if you kill it, just
make another!

When you make a batch of Go-To Dough,
pinch off a piece the size of a golf ball, add it
to a jar with a lid, and leave out at room temperature. After 3 days, feed it by adding ¼ cup
[60 ml] water and ¼ cup [72 g] flour and
mix. It should resemble very thick pancake
batter—add more water or flour it it's too tight
or too loose. The next day, you can begin
using it as starter.

Store in the refrigerator and feed it every
week by removing half of its volume (about
¼ cup [60 ml]), known as discard, and repeating the feeding process from above. The
longer you keep it, the tangier it gets.

Use the discard by adding it to dishes like the
Smoked Fish and Squash Blossom Pancake
with Crispy Honey Chili Oil (page 173) or
regular pancakes, biscuits, and cakes to give
them a bit more spring and a deeper flavor
during the oven rise.

Toppings

**SPICED FINISHING OIL (PAGE 117) AND
EVERYTHING DUKKAH MIX (PAGE 109)**

**AVOCADO-CUMIN BUTTER (PAGE 69)
AND SESAME, CRANBERRY SEED, AND
SAFFLOWER GOMASIO (PAGE 106)**

**DRIZZLE WITH VANILLA OIL (PAGE 119) AND
TOP WITH SLICED SUPER-RIPE TOMATOES
AND FLAKY SALT**

SAVORY LEMON FOCACCIA

Makes one 6 by 9 in [15 by 23 cm] focaccia

The combination of lemon and vanilla is one of my favorites. (Have you ever tried adding vanilla to your lemonade? You should!) With this dish, I add thinly sliced lemon, a drizzle of vanilla oil, and lots of flaky salt. The lemon slices get cooked and become tacky and crunchy, tart and salty, which contrasts with the soft, puffy focaccia.

1 recipe Go-To Dough (page 138)
2 Tbsp Vanilla Oil (page 119)
½ organic unwaxed lemon, thinly sliced
½ tsp flaky or coarse sea salt

Prepare the dough according to the Go-To Dough recipe (page 138), and take it through the first rise. Line a 6 by 9 in [15 by 23 cm] pan with parchment and grease the parchment. Spread the dough in the pan and let proof on the counter for 1 hour if the dough is cold or 30 minutes if the dough is warm, until it doubles in size again.

Preheat the oven to 400°F [200°C].

With your fingers, make dimples throughout the surface of the dough and top with the vanilla oil, lemon slices, and salt. Bake for approximately 20 minutes, until golden brown. Focaccia is best the day it is baked.

CHEESE BISCUITS WITH GUAVA JAM

Makes 6 biscuits

This is an homage to a very traditional Caribbean cheese and guava jam dish. I use blue cheese to flavor my biscuits, which I know isn't a favorite of many people. But I promise: This biscuit has a bold, cheesy flavor without the blue cheese funk. Mixing ¼ cup [60 ml] sourdough mother in with the buttermilk, if you have it, makes them even more fluffy and flavorful.

2 cups [280 g] all-purpose flour

2 tsp baking powder

½ tsp baking soda

1 tsp salt

¾ cup [170 g] cold butter, cubed

2 oz [55 g] cold blue cheese, crumbled

½ cup [120 ml] buttermilk

2 Tbsp melted butter or olive oil, for brushing

Butter, at room temperature, for serving

Guava Jam (page 101), for serving

Preheat the oven 400°F [200°C]. Line a baking sheet with parchment paper.

IF USING A FOOD PROCESSOR: In a food processor, add the flour, baking powder, baking soda, and salt and pulse a few times. Add the cold butter and cheese and pulse until they're cut into pea-size pieces. Transfer to a medium bowl and drizzle in the buttermilk, slowly mixing the dough while drizzling, until a dough forms.

IF MIXING BY HAND: In a bowl, add the flour, baking powder, baking soda, and salt and whisk to combine. Add the cold butter and flatten each piece of butter with your fingertips. Add the cheese, stir to combine, then drizzle in the buttermilk, slowly mixing the dough while drizzling, until a dough forms.

Turn out the dough onto a clean work surface and push the dough together. Using a rolling pin, create a 1 in [2.5 cm] thick rectangle. Cut into fours by cutting once crosswise and once lengthwise and stack the quarters. Roll the stack out again to create a 1 in [2.5 cm] thick rectangle, making sure your edges are clean and straight. Repeat twice more; this gives the biscuits flaky and delicious layers. Cut the dough into 6 pieces.

Transfer the biscuits to the prepared baking sheet. Freeze for 15 minutes.

Remove from the freezer, brush with the melted butter, and bake until golden brown, 25 to 30 minutes. Serve warm with room-temperature butter and guava jam.

Baked biscuits are best the day of. Make only as many as you need and store the remaining unbaked biscuits in a lidded container or plastic bag in the freezer for 3 months.

OAT-DATE-TAHINI COOKIES

Makes 12 cookies

This is a modern ode to my favorite cookie: oatmeal raisin. The plump dates stand in for the raisins, adding a special jammy texture, while the addition of tahini gives it a rich, savory note that cuts through the sweetness. These cookies are perfect for breakfast or a midday treat with tea.

¾ cup [105 g] all-purpose flour
2 Tbsp mandarin powder or other fruit powder (see page 115)
½ tsp ground allspice
¼ tsp baking soda
¼ tsp baking powder
¼ tsp salt
½ cup [100 g] granulated cane sugar
1 Tbsp molasses
½ cup [115 g] unsalted butter, at room temperature
2 Tbsp tahini
1 egg
1 tsp vanilla extract
1 cup [80 g] rolled oats
10 dates, chilled, pitted, and torn into quarters or sixths

Preheat the oven to 350°F [180°C]. Line a baking sheet with parchment paper.

In a small bowl, whisk together the flour, 1 Tbsp of the mandarin powder, allspice, baking soda, baking powder, and salt. Set aside.

In the bowl of a stand mixer fitted with a paddle attachment or in a bowl with a hand mixer, combine the brown sugar, molasses, butter, and tahini. Beat on medium-high speed until smooth and fluffy, about 5 minutes, stopping midway to scrape down the bowl.

Add the egg and vanilla and beat for 1 minute. Add the flour mixture and mix in by hand. Once almost all combined, add the oats and then fold in half of the dates.

Using a 1½ in [4 cm] scooper, scoop dough onto the prepared baking sheet, leaving enough space for them to spread. Dot each cookie with two or three pieces of the remaining dates and press in slightly. Bake for 15 to 17 minutes or until light golden, rotating the pan once during baking.

Pull the baking sheet from the oven and immediately slam it onto the counter twice to deflate the cookies. This technique makes for exceptionally dense centers and crunchy tops. Using a fine-mesh sieve, dust the cookies with the remaining mandarin powder. Let the cookies cool completely before removing from the baking sheet. Store in an airtight container at room temperature for 2 days.

WARM CARROT-ALMOND TEA CAKE WITH CINNAMON TURMERIC HONEY GHEE

Makes one 9 in [23 cm] round or 6 in [15 cm] square

Sugar and spice will cure many things. But more so, cinnamon and other hard spices provide so many powerful benefits that the body needs. Cinnamon is known to lower blood pressure, which is probably not surprising. The moment I smell cinnamon, I'm instantly chill—it's like seeing a reliable old friend.

1 to 2 Tbsp seeds, such as sesame, hemp, or flax (optional)

2 cups [280 g] grated carrot

1 cup [140 g] grated apple or pineapple

3 large eggs

¾ cup [160 ml] extra-virgin olive oil

¼ cup [60 g] yogurt

½ cup [100 g] granulated cane sugar

1 tsp vanilla extract

2 cups [280 g] all-purpose flour

¼ cup [20 g] desiccated coconut

¼ cup [35 g] sliced almonds

2 tsp ground cinnamon

1 tsp baking soda

½ tsp ground ginger

¼ tsp turmeric

1 tsp salt

Pinch ground black pepper

Cinnamon Turmeric Honey Ghee (page 71), for serving

Preheat the oven to 350°F [180°C]. Grease a 9 in [23 cm] cake pan. If desired, sprinkle the pan with the seeds for a crunchy coating that also helps the cake not stick to the pan.

In a large bowl, add the carrot, apple, eggs, olive oil, yogurt, sugar, and vanilla. Mix well to combine.

In a separate medium bowl, add the flour, coconut, almonds, cinnamon, baking soda, ginger, turmeric, salt, and pepper. Mix well to combine. Stir the dry ingredients into the wet ingredients until combined, and then pour into the prepared pan.

Bake until the center is fully set, 1 to 1½ hours.

Let cool for 15 minutes in the pan, then invert onto a plate. Serve with a slather of the ghee. Store well-wrapped leftovers for 2 days at room temperature.

SNACKS

Sometimes we're hungry and all we need is just a little bite of something to pull us through. The act of pausing, composing a small bite, and taking a break to nourish ourselves is an art, an act of self-care. When we crave a snack, it's because our body is calling out for a little nourishment, and the solution can be as simple as a piece of toast with good butter or eating a few briny pickles directly from the jar. But this section is all about making intentional bites with big flavor for your afternoon break, or to share with others as appetizers or sides to a lunch or dinner. They're quick to prepare, don't involve a lot of cooking, and come together effortlessly with items you already have in your pantry or fridge.

QUICK ADAPTOGEN MOKA POT SIPPING BROTH

Makes 1 cup [240 ml]

This super-charged shot takes minutes to make and contains essential minerals and adaptogens. The moka pot, an Italian espresso maker, uses steam to create pressure ideal for an extraction. As the hot pressurized water moves up to the top chamber, it extracts from the ingredients in the filter funnel. It's great when you're sick and not in the mood to eat but need nourishment. It's also key when you need a super quick stock or a broth for a dish, or to add flavor to dishes like risotto or steamed greens.

1 cup [240 ml] filtered or spring water

2 tsp shoyu or soy sauce

2 dried shiitake mushrooms, thinly sliced or coarsely ground

3 Tbsp Super-Powered Powder (page 114)

1 Tbsp nori flakes

1 tsp grated fresh ginger or ½ tsp ground ginger

Pinch chili powder (optional)

Salt

Using a 6 oz [180 ml] moka pot (cleaned well to remove any coffee odors), add the water and shoyu to the bottom chamber. Make sure it doesn't go higher than the piston. Top with the filter funnel. Add the remaining ingredients to the funnel in layers: first the ground shiitake mushroom, then the Super-Powered Powder, followed by the nori flakes and ginger, and finished with the chili powder (if using). Pat down the ingredients, twist on the top chamber, and place over low heat. Once it stops gurgling, about 5 minutes, remove from the heat. Season with salt to taste, and if it's too strong, add a little bit of hot water.

CORN AND CHICKPEA FRITTERS WITH GINGER-GARLIC MOJO

Makes 16 fritters

This dish is a cross between panisse (a chickpea flour fritter) and fried polenta, with little bit of surullitos (Caribbean cornmeal sticks) thrown in. I love the flavor a good masa gives. It's perfect accompanied by the garlic mojo I've taken directly from my childhood.

½ cup [65 g] chickpea flour

¼ cup [35 g] masa (hominy flour) or fine cornmeal

½ tsp salt

Pinch chili powder

1 cup [30 ml] filtered or spring water

Neutral oil, such as sunflower, grapeseed, safflower, or rice bran, for frying

Ginger-Garlic Mojo (page 50), for serving

Have a 6 by 9 in [15 by 23 cm] baking pan next to the stove so you can pour the batter in before it sets after cooking.

In a medium, heavy-bottom pot, whisk together the chickpea flour, masa, salt, and chili powder. Make a well in the center and add the water gradually, whisking continuously until the batter is smooth. Cook the mixture over medium heat, whisking constantly to prevent scorching. It'll go from milky to almost translucent as it cooks. Once the batter starts to separate from the bottom of the pan, after about 6 minutes, spread the mixture evenly in the baking pan. Let cool on the counter for 10 minutes. Cover with parchment or plastic wrap and refrigerate for 1 hour.

Invert the mixture from the pan onto a cutting board. Cut it in half lengthwise, and then cut crosswise into four pieces. Then cut each piece diagonally, so you have sixteen triangles in total.

Add the oil to a skillet or sauté pan to a depth of ¼ in [6 mm] and heat to an optimum temperature of 350°F [180°C]. Fry the fritters in batches until golden brown, about 4 minutes per side, and transfer to a rack or paper towel–lined plate to drain. Serve hot with the mojo.

HIPPIE SANDWICH

Makes 1 sandwich

This veggie sandwich is endlessly customizable, but the main components include a protein, something crunchy, something vinegary, a delicious spread, and sprouts (always sprouts!). Feel free to play around with swapping out your ingredients or adjusting their amounts; for example, add crunch with cucumber, lettuce, shredded carrot, or radish instead of jicama. Swap out the Cheddar for hummus or goat cheese. Feeling a little spicy? Add a shake of Fermented Hot Sauce (page 80) or thinly sliced fresh jalapeño.

2 slices semi-dense fresh bread like focaccia (page 139) or whole wheat

2 Tbsp Green Goddess Yogurt (page 39)

2 to 3 thin slices jicama

1 slice Cheddar

2 to 3 Tbsp something pickled or fermented, such as sauerkraut, pickled peppers, store-bought kimchi, or pickles (see Note)

Generous handful sprouts (see page 178)

Olive oil, for drizzling

Vinegar, for drizzling

Salt and chili powder or black pepper

Fermented Hot Sauce (page 80) or sliced chiles (optional)

Build the sandwich on one slice of bread, layering the ingredients: spread a thick layer of yogurt, add the jicama and Cheddar, then the pickles. Top with the sprouts, then drizzle with oil and vinegar. Add salt and chili powder to taste. Add a spicy component (if using), top with the second slice of bread, give it a good smash, and enjoy.

NOTE: Pickled things that work well here include Cucumber and Dulse Pickle (page 76), Chile-Mushroom Pickle (page 77), Dried Red Berry and Beet Pickle (page 77), Pickled Mustard Seed (page 78), Turmeric Fennel and Onion Condiment (page 79), and Red Cabbage and Nigella Relish (page 80).

STUFFED CRISPY GRAPE LEAVES WITH CURRY LEAF YOGURT AND PINE NUTS

Serves 2 to 4

When I was younger, dolmas were so mysterious. As I grew older and my palate evolved, I became hooked on these briny, dense, big-flavor bites. I find them so beautiful, each one wrapped by hand and cared for before being cooked and landing in your mouth.

This dish offers all the wonders of a dolma with a modern twist. It uses leftover rice or grains and is a great option for a snack or light lunch when you just can't bring yourself to make yet another grain salad or stir-fried rice. The barberries or currants give it a wonderful balance of sweet and salty, and I love the texture of the fried and crisped-up grape leaves.

If you don't have or like grape leaves, this filling can also be used to stuff a whole fish, calamari body, or hollowed-out zucchini and baked.

2 Tbsp dried barberries or currants

16 brined grape leaves

1 cup [120 g] cooked rice

¼ cup [30 g] crumbled feta

2 Tbsp roasted pine nuts (see page 105)

1 to 2 Tbsp neutral oil, such as sunflower, grapeseed, safflower, or rice bran, for frying

Curry Leaf Yogurt (page 37), for serving

In a small bowl, cover the barberries with hot water to rehydrate them and let sit for approximately 10 minutes.

cont'd

Remove the grape leaves from the brine and rinse under cold water. Lay them flat on a rack or a clean towel to dry.

In a medium bowl, add the rice, feta, and pine nuts. With a slotted spoon, scoop out the dried fruit, reserving the liquid, and add the fruit to the rice. Mix well. Press the mixture tightly together with your hands; if it doesn't stick together, add a little of the dried fruit liquid, 1 Tbsp at a time, until it does.

On a clean work surface, lay two grape leaves, one pointing up and one pointing down, overlapping at the base by ½ in [13 mm]. Place 2 Tbsp of the rice mixture in the center. Fold in half. Carefully transfer to a baking sheet, repeat with the remaining leaves, and refrigerate the stuffed leaves for 1 hour.

Add the oil to a skillet or sauté pan over medium heat. Add the stuffed grape leaf pouches, being careful not to crowd the pan. Let crisp up undisturbed for 3 to 4 minutes and then flip and cook for 3 to 4 minutes longer, until crispy on both sides. Serve with the yogurt.

A PRIMER FOR A PERFECT POACHED EGG

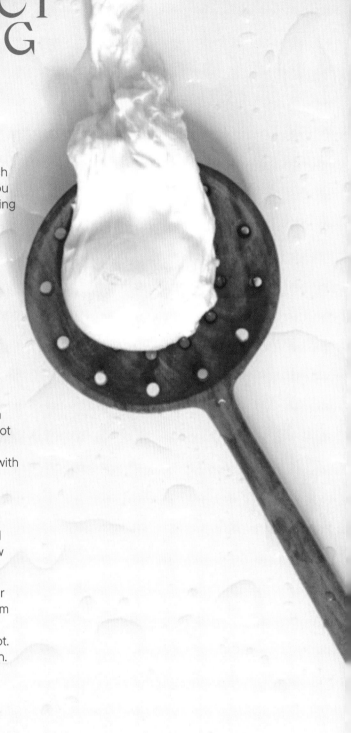

Making the perfect poached egg is something a brunch cook becomes very good at. With a big-enough pot, you can poach twenty-four eggs at a time. There is something so beautiful to me about how the bubbles that come up from the bottom of the pot sculpt the egg. Once the egg whites solidify with the heat, what's left is the perfect teardrop shape, a moment suspended in time.

To make the perfect poached egg, fill a pot that is 5 in [12 cm] or more deep with water. To achieve the sculptural teardrop shape, the eggs need to have a bit of room as they plunge into the water.

Bring the water to a boil. It's also important to achieve the perfect boil for the perfect poach. The perfect boil has a gentle gurgling—not so gentle that the egg sinks and sticks flat on the bottom, but also not too rapid of a boil that the egg bops around and potentially bursts. Not unlike using a gas pedal of a car to go faster or slower, play around with the heat so that you get comfortable with controlling the boil.

Once the perfect boil is achieved, add a splash of distilled vinegar (3 Tbsp for every 4 qt [3.8 L] of water) and a five-finger pinch of salt to the water. You can also add 1 Tbsp ground turmeric to turn the eggs a festive yellow color if you wish.

When the environment is right, give the water a light stir with a spoon. Now, drop in the eggs. You can crack them carefully into the water, or for more control, first crack it into a small shallow bowl, then slide the egg into the pot. Set a timer for 2 minutes from the time you drop them in.

Check the bubbles and adjust the heat if needed. The bubbles should float up and sculpt the egg whites.

Carefully remove the eggs with a slotted spoon, and use immediately.

TURKISH EGGS WITH CRISPY HONEY CHILI OIL

Serves 2 to 4

I learned this dish from a good friend and co-chef of mine. At its core, it's a flavorful yogurt that is then topped with an egg and crispy chili oil. It's always been a brunch hit in most of the restaurants I've worked at.

1 garlic clove

1 Tbsp fresh lemon juice

½ cup [120 g] strained yogurt

2 to 4 teardrop-shaped poached eggs (see page 157)

Swirl of finishing oil, such as Crispy Honey Chili Oil (page 118)

4 slices of chunky toast (sourdough or challah are good options)

In a bowl, add the garlic and lemon juice. Let it cure for 5 minutes, then mix in the strained yogurt.

Divide the yogurt among plates, top each with a poached egg, and finish with a drizzle of oil. Serve with chunky toast for dipping.

VEGAN NACHOS

Serves 2 to 4

Nachos are an interactive experience—we have to work for that perfect bite with all the components—but it's also a dish that progresses along a timeline. Everything starts off hot and crispy at first, and then slowly the dish starts to get saturated in some areas. You now have a mix of soft and crunchy chips, and so starts the searching for the bit that has all the ingredients and all the textures.

One 12 oz [340 g] bag tortilla chips

1½ cups [360 g] Cuban Beans (see page 212)

1 recipe Cashew Queso (page 54)

2 avocados, peeled, pitted, and mashed
with fresh lime juice and salt to taste

½ cup [75 g] Turmeric Fennel and Onion Condiment (page 79)

1 watermelon radish, thinly sliced

Pico de Gallo (recipe follows), for serving

Fermented Hot Sauce (page 80), for serving

Arrange half of the chips on a serving platter. Dot with some of the beans and drizzle with some of the queso. Scatter some of the mashed avocado, fennel and onion condiment, radish slices, and pico de gallo over the chips. Repeat, making a second layer, and top with the hot sauce and reserved cilantro leaves from the pico de gallo. Serve immediately.

PICO DE GALLO

½ white onion

2 ripe Roma-style tomatoes

1 jalapeño, seeded

½ bunch cilantro, leaves separated from the stems

Juice of 3 limes

1 Tbsp salt

Finely chop the onion, tomatoes, jalapeño, and cilantro stems (reserve the leaves) and transfer to a bowl. Add the lime juice and salt and allow to sit for 15 minutes. Coarsely chop the cilantro leaves, add half to the pico de gallo, and reserve the other half for garnishing the nachos. Use immediately.

NIGELLA CAULIFLOWER FRITTERS WITH PICKLED MUSTARD SEED SAUCE

Serves 2 to 4

Nigella has big medicinal value—as the saying goes, nigella cures everything but death. It has a smoky, distinct flavor with notes of cumin and onion, and tastes like nothing else. You can make this dish with whatever cruciferous vegetables you have on hand. The beauty is that before frying, you dip them in a batter spiked with nigella seeds for extra crunch and flavor. Every good fritter needs a dipping sauce. Sometimes, I'll just whip something up from some mayonnaise I have in the fridge, but every now and then I like these with a luxe, rich, velvety hollandaise.

1 lb [455 g] whole cauliflower, leaves attached, or Romanesco, broccoli, or cabbage

½ cup [70 g] rice flour

½ cup [70 g] all-purpose flour

2 tsp nigella seeds

1 tsp baking powder

1 tsp salt

Pinch chili powder

2 cups [480 ml] filtered water

Neutral oil, such as sunflower, grapeseed, or rice bran, for frying

Mayonnaise (page 58) or Hollandaise (page 59)

Pickled Mustard Seed (page 78)

Prepare the cauliflower by keeping 2 in [5 cm] of the stalk and cutting lengthwise into long, thin slices.

In a large bowl, whisk together the rice flour, all-purpose flour, nigella seeds, baking powder, salt, and chili powder. Whisk in the water.

Add the oil to a skillet or sauté pan to a depth of ¼ in [6 mm] and heat to 350°F [180°C].

Dip the florets into the batter and fry until golden brown, 3 to 4 minutes on each side. Work in batches so as not to crowd the pan. Drain on a paper towel–lined plate.

In a bowl, add the mayonnaise or hollandaise and swirl in the mustard seed. Serve with the fritters.

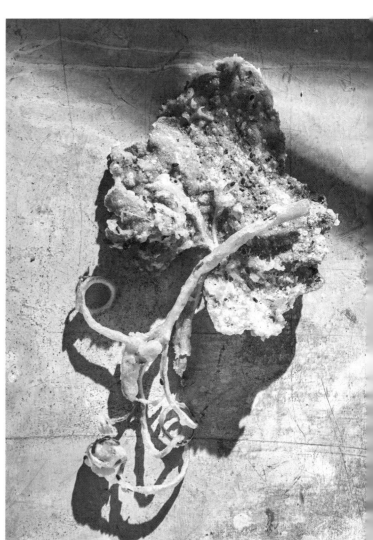

DAL FRITTERS WITH LECHE DE TIGRE

Makes 14 fritters

In essence, this easy and satisfying little fritter is a twist on falafel, swapping out chickpeas for red dal. Enjoy them as is or stuffed in a pita or baguette with loads of fresh herbs, pickles, and your favorite sauce. I use Leche de Tigre here, but this is delicious with many sauces, including tahini, hummus, or yogurt sauces topped with a drizzle of chili oil.

½ cup [100 g] split red lentils (dal)

1 cup [240 ml] hot filtered water

½ onion, thinly sliced

¼ cup [10 g] coarsely chopped herbs such as cilantro, dill, or parsley

½ tsp salt

2 Tbsp chickpea flour or almond flour

½ tsp baking soda

½ tsp whole cumin seed

2 Tbsp neutral oil, such as sunflower, grapeseed, safflower, or rice bran, for frying

¼ cup [5 g] chopped cilantro

1 recipe Leche de Tigre (page 49)

Add the dal to a medium bowl and cover with water from the tap. Swish around and drain. Repeat twice. Add the hot filtered water to cover the dal and let sit for 1 hour.

Strain the dal and add it to a food processor along with the salt. Process until it resembles a chunky purée, scraping down the sides midway through. Transfer to a small bowl and stir in the onion, herbs, chickpea flour, baking soda, and cumin seed.

In a heavy frying or cast-iron pan over medium-high heat, warm the oil until it reaches 350°F [180°C]. Carefully drop in 1 Tbsp batter at a time and fry until golden brown, 3 to 4 minutes per side. Remove to a rack or paper towel–lined plate to drain.

In a bowl, mix the chopped cilantro into the leche de tigre and serve immediately alongside the fritters. Leftover batter can be kept in the refrigerator for 2 to 3 days.

ROASTED EGGPLANT DIP WITH SALSA VERDE AND TAHINI

Serves 2 to 4

This is one of those crowd favorites that's also super easy and quick to make. Once the eggplant has been roasted, you just mash everything and top it with salsa verde and tahini. Diners tear a piece of warm pita and dip it into the eggplant. It's so satisfying, very visual, and one of the easiest dishes in this entire book.

1 large eggplant
½ cup [120 g] Salsa Verde (page 64)
2 Tbsp Green Tahini (page 54) or plain tahini, thinned with 1 Tbsp hot water
Extra-virgin olive oil, for drizzling
Crunchy sea salt, for sprinkling
Flatbread, pita, or challah, for serving

Preheat the oven to 450°F [230°C]. Grease a baking sheet.

Halve the eggplant lengthwise. Place the eggplant cut-side down on the prepared baking sheet. Bake until soft, approximately 20 minutes.

To serve, transfer the eggplant cut-side up to a platter. Smash the flesh with a fork. Dollop with the salsa and tahini and swirl, then drizzle with the olive oil and sprinkle with sea salt. Serve with flatbread.

MAPLE CHICORIES WITH CHILE-MUSHROOM PICKLE TOAST

Serves 2

Magic happens when you coat chicories in a bit of maple syrup (or other sweet syrup) and then grill it. The syrup balances the bitterness of chicories in a really wonderful way, and the flavor profile is perfect for a cozy winter snack. Add a schmear of goat or ricotta cheese to the toast for added satisfaction.

1 small head bitter chicory, such as radicchio, leaves separated
1 Tbsp maple syrup, honey, agave, or rice syrup
Pinch salt
¼ tsp chili powder
2 thick slices of your favorite bread
Extra-virgin olive oil, for the toast
¼ cup [55 g] Chile-Mushroom Pickle (page 77)
Crunchy sea salt, for sprinkling

In a large bowl, combine the chicory leaves, maple syrup, salt, and chili powder. Using tongs, toss well to coat and let sit for 5 minutes.

Toast your bread, and then drizzle it with olive oil while it's still warm.

In a dry cast-iron skillet or grill pan over medium-high heat, add the chicory leaves in batches so as not to crowd the pan and let cook undisturbed until the leaves are slightly charred, about 1 minute on each side. Pile the chicory leaves onto the toast and top with the mushroom pickle. Finish with a hearty drizzle of olive oil and a sprinkling of crunchy sea salt.

ANATOMY

of a Toast

UNI BUTTER (PAGE 70) TOAST WITH SALMON ROE

NORI PESTO (PAGE 64) TOAST WITH DRESSED RADISH AND SPROUTS

TOAST WITH GRIBICHE (PAGE 59) AND TURMERIC FENNEL FERMENT

CHILE-MUSHROOM PICKLE (PAGE 77) TOAST
WITH FRIED EGG AND HONEY CHILI CRISP

RASPBERRY JAM TOAST WITH TAHINI, HONEY, AND SESAME OIL

CABBAGE NIGELLA FERMENT

COCONUT YOGURT PAPADUM

LECHE DE TIGRE CEVICHE ON TOSTADA

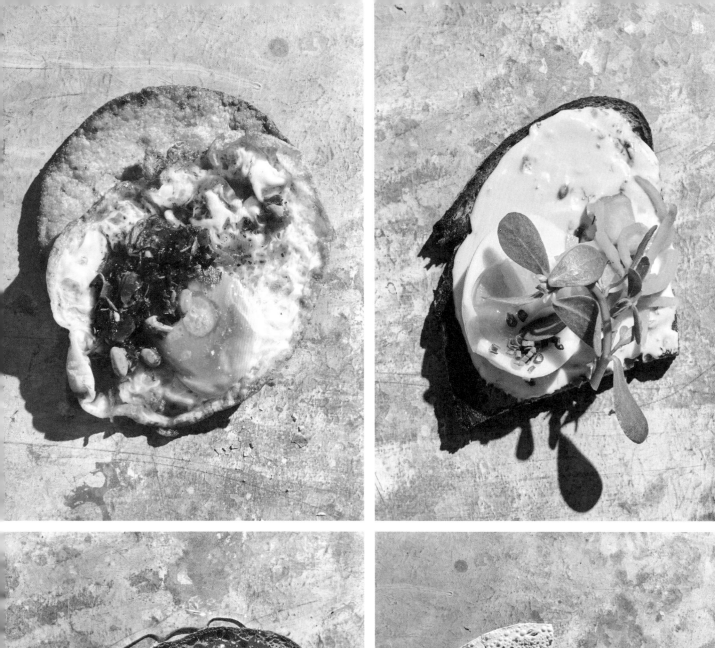
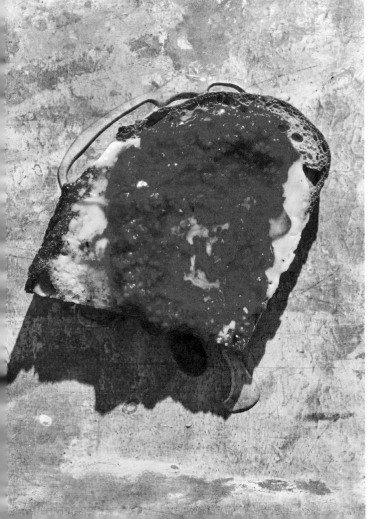
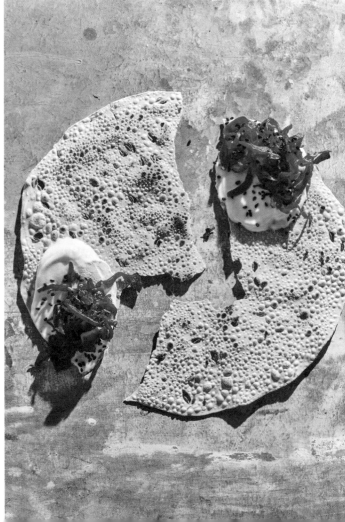

SMOKED FISH AND SQUASH BLOSSOM PANCAKE WITH CRISPY HONEY CHILI OIL

Serves 2 to 4

This is another ode to my Caribbean childhood and the famous beachside cuchifrito, or fried food, stands of Puerto Rico. This dish is essentially a bacalaíto, which is made with imported salt cod, but the smoked trout we get here in New York is so wonderful that I often swap it in instead. In the summertime, the delicate squash blossoms look so pretty while providing a pop of color within the pancakes.

1 cup [140 g] all-purpose flour

1 cup [240 ml] filtered water

1 tsp salt

3 oz [85 g] smoked white fish

2 green onions, thinly sliced

Neutral oil, such as sunflower, grapeseed, safflower, or rice bran, for frying

6 squash blossoms (see Note)

Crispy Honey Chili Oil (page 118), for serving

In a large bowl, whisk together the flour, water, and salt to make a batter. Add the fish and green onions and stir to combine.

In a cast-iron skillet or sauté pan over medium heat, drizzle in some neutral oil. Pour enough batter into the skillet to coat the bottom. Dot with the petals of the squash blossom. Cook until golden brown, 3 to 5 minutes. Flip and cook the other side for 3 to 5 minutes, until golden brown. Transfer to a cutting board and cut into wedges. Serve with the chili oil.

NOTE: If it's not squash flower season, you can substitute the blossoms with steamed cabbage leaves, cut into 2 in [5 cm] strips.

SALTED COD PUFFS WITH GREEN OLIVE AIOLI

Makes 12 puffs

I fry only during the summer when I can open the windows wide. This little fritter does require some prep, but it's such a special apéro dish for when you have people over that it's worth the effort.

8 oz [230 g] salted cod
½ cup [120 ml] milk
½ medium onion
1 large russet potato, peeled and cubed
1 egg
1 garlic clove, minced or grated
Pinch chili powder
¼ cup [35 g] all-purpose flour
2 tsp baking powder
⅓ cup [45 g] bread crumbs
Neutral oil, such as sunflower, grapeseed, or rice bran, for frying
10 fresh sage leaves
½ cup [120 g] Green Olive Aioli (page 58), optional
¼ cup [30 g] roasted pecans (see page 105)

Soak the cod in cool water overnight in the refrigerator. Remove the cod and discard the liquid.

In a medium pot over low heat, add the cod, milk, and onion. Slowly warm to a low simmer and cook at a low gurgle for 20 minutes, stirring intermittently. Remove the cod to a large bowl to cool, reserving the milk. Add the potato to the milk and simmer until tender, about 15 minutes, then drain.

Add the cooked potatoes to the bowl with the cod, followed by the egg, garlic, and chili powder, and mix well. In a small bowl, mix together the flour and baking powder, then fold it into the cod mixture. Cool the mixture, roll into balls, and roll each in the bread crumbs to coat.

Add the oil to a small heavy-bottom pot to a depth of 1 in [2.5 cm] and heat over medium-high to 350°F [180°C]. Working in batches, scoop small spoonfuls of the batter into the oil, making sure not to crowd them, and fry until golden, 3 to 4 minutes on each side. Drain on a paper towel–lined plate.

Carefully fry the sage leaves one at a time for a few seconds and drain. Serve the puffs hot with the fried sage, aioli, and roasted pecans (if using).

SALADS

I am a big fan of the salad lifestyle. Salads can be, and should be, full meals, and if you ask me, salads are perfect for breakfast, lunch, or dinner. A salad in the morning always puts me in a great mood for the rest of the day. Raw, fresh, crunchy, bright, juicy, salty, and light, salads have always been my power food. They contain vitamins and are brimming with life force energy your body absorbs and processes easily. I've always had multiple salads on my restaurant menus. And after making many salads for many people, I've learned that the key to a delicious salad is knowing the texture of the ingredients. If you are using leafy greens that are sturdy and dense, such as kale and chicories, be sure to toss them well. If you are using delicate vegetables or making a composed salad, drizzle the dressing. When people start their cooking journey, they are often most comfortable making salads because they are easy to customize and make your own. Salads leave plenty of space for creativity and are the perfect place to practice combining your pantry staples in new and different ways.

SPROUTING

The ideal way of eating beans, in my opinion, is picking them fresh off the vine in summer and tossing them into a pot of aromatics with enough water to cover and a glug of oil. They cook in minutes, are full of flavor, and are easier to digest. But for the rest of the year, I recommend sprouting your dried beans before you use them to replicate the benefits of eating them fresh off the vine. Someone once told me that years and years ago all cooks sprouted their dried beans before cooking them, and I believe it. You can also sprout whole grains such as farro for similar benefits.

When cooking with sprouted beans, allow for the sprouts to grow less than ⅛ in [3 mm] before using. With certain beans, the skins detach, making them even easier to digest. To remove them completely, add the beans to a bowl of water and gently rub them—the skins will rise to the top, making it easy to scoop them out. When sprouting seeds, grow their sprouts longer and eat those raw, as these microsprouts are full of vital energy.

The basic sprouting process, whether for beans, seeds, or grains, requires a soak. Once drained, they'll need to be rinsed twice a day until they sprout. There are a few ways of storing them while they sprout: stacking sprouting trays you can buy or using Mason jars. If you don't have either, you can simply put them on a tray or colander in between two paper towels, continuing to wet the towels to ensure they stay damp throughout the sprouting process. The more you water, the more plump your sprouts will be.

I try to make a habit of sprouting beans every two weeks so that I always have a supply on hand. If you're not planning to use them right away, you can freeze the whole pot of beans (without draining), to be used in the future.

Sprouting Beans

Rinse the beans and soak in filtered water overnight. Pick out any broken or shriveled beans. Transfer to a sprouting tray or glass jar. Rinse the beans twice a day. Within 2 or 3 days, they'll begin sprouting. Add to a large pot and cover with filtered water by 2 in [5 cm]. Add aromatics, such as whole garlic, whole chiles, ½ onion, and a pinch of salt. Sprouted beans cook in a fraction of the time it takes for whole, dried beans. Small beans can take 10 to 15 minutes and larger ones 20 minutes. Check on them often while cooking.

Sprouting Grains

Rinse unhulled grains and soak in filtered water for 4 hours. Rinse and transfer to a sprouting tray or glass jar. Rinse the grains twice a day, once in the morning and once in the evening, removing any gelatinous skin that may form. Depending on the warmth of the environment, you'll see the grains sprout within 2 to 3 days. Cook sprouted whole grains as you would pasta, in a pot of salted boiling water until tender, about 10 minutes, then drain in a colander or sieve.

Sprouting Seeds

My favorite seeds to sprout are fenugreek, chia, pumpkin, and sunflower. Rinse hulled or unhulled raw seeds and soak in filtered water for 1 hour. Rinse and transfer to a sprouting tray or glass jar. Rinse the seeds once a day, removing any gelatinous skin that forms. Depending on the warmth of the environment, they'll sprout within a day or two. Serve uncooked sprouted seeds topped on salads or tucked into sandwiches.

RHUBARB, NAPA CABBAGE, AND WATERMELON RADISH SALAD WITH BIG FLAVOR DRESSING

Serves 2 to 4

I love rhubarb! Most of us recognize it in sweet applications, but rhubarb has a savory element to it. Because of its tartness, it goes great with crunchy vegetables and rich nuts or cheese to balance its pungency. I love its color and the surprising effect of serving it in a savory way. A bright dressing like the Citronette (page 45) pairs very well with it, but I especially love the Big Flavor Dressing (page 48) with this, too. If you must substitute the rhubarb, try celery.

1 rhubarb stalk, thinly sliced

2 tsp granulated cane sugar

¼ cup [60 ml] Big Flavor Dressing (page 48)

¼ head napa cabbage, leaves cut into 2 in [5 cm] squares

1 small watermelon radish, thinly sliced

¼ cup [35 g] roasted pistachios (see page 105), coarsely chopped

Pinch of dulse flakes (optional)

In a medium bowl, combine the rhubarb and sugar. Let marinate for 10 minutes, then add the dressing. Mix in the cabbage and radish.

Topping with pistachios and dulse (if using) is a colorful and textural addition but also balances the tartness. Divide among two to four plates and serve.

NAPA CABBAGE, COCONUT, AND PECAN SALAD WITH PECAN-COCONUT DRESSING

Serves 2

This is a crisp, clean, nourishing salad with unexpected ingredients, such as cabbage and fresh coconut, that help you think outside the box of what a salad can be.

½ cup [60 g] roasted pecans (see page 105)

¼ head napa cabbage, cut into bite-size pieces

½ cup [40 g] sliced fresh coconut

¼ cup [60 ml] Pecan-Coconut Dressing (page 49)

Leaves from ½ bunch cilantro, chopped

1 Tbsp desiccated unsweetened coconut, for topping

In a bowl, combine the pecans, cabbage, and fresh coconut. Add the dressing and toss to coat. Divide the salad between two plates and garnish with the chopped cilantro and desiccated coconut. Serve immediately.

ENDIVE AND PARSNIP SALAD WITH PISTACHIO, BLUE CHEESE, AND CITRONETTE

Serves 2 to 4

This winter salad was a crowd favorite from the menu at my restaurant Navy. The neutral flavor and crunch of the endive, the spice and sweetness of the parsnip, the richness of the pistachios, the saltiness of the blue cheese, and the acidity of the citronette tick all the boxes on the flavor checklist.

2 parsnips, scrubbed and sliced crosswise ⅛ in [3 mm] thick
¼ cup [60 ml] vegetable oil
½ tsp agave, honey, or maple syrup
Pinch kosher salt
Pinch chili powder
4 small white endives, leaves separated
4 small white turnips, trimmed and thinly sliced on a mandoline
4 oz [115 g] blue cheese, frozen for 20 minutes and shaved with a peeler
¼ cup [60 ml] Citronette (page 45)
¼ cup [35 g] roasted pistachios (see page 105), chopped
Flaky sea salt

Preheat the oven to 400°F [200°C].

On a rimmed baking sheet, toss the parsnips with the oil and agave and season with kosher salt and chili powder. Roast, turning once, until the parsnips are tender, about 15 minutes. Cool completely before assembling the salad.

Divide the parsnips, endive leaves, turnips, and blue cheese among two to four plates. Drizzle with the dressing, top with the pistachios, and season with flaky sea salt. Serve immediately.

CHICORIES AND SEAWEEDS

Serves 4

Confession time: I am over kale. But that doesn't mean I don't want something that gives me that same regenerative feeling. I have taken to chicories, which I love during the wintertime because there is a great selection. To them, I added three types of sea vegetables: hijiki, aonori, and spirulina, plus two of my favorite greens, escarole and watercress, to end up with a beautiful green, leafy salad that hits all the marks and gives each cell of my body that same happy feeling that kale does.

½ cup [70 g] roasted hazelnuts (see page 105)

Grapeseed oil

Salt

Chili powder

1 head of escarole, torn into bite-size pieces (about 8 cups [190 g])

2 Tbsp hijiki, reconstituted in water

¾ cup [180 ml] Honey-Miso Dressing (page 45)

1 bunch watercress, leaves and stems cut into 2 in [5 cm] pieces

2 avocados, peeled, pitted, and sliced

¼ cup [35 g] Seaweed Gomasio (page 108)

Spirulina-Lemon Powder a.k.a. Magic Powder (page 111)

In a small bowl, lightly dress the hazelnuts with a drizzle of grapeseed oil, a sprinkle of salt, and a small bit of chili powder.

In a large bowl, combine the escarole and hijiki and add half the miso dressing. Massage the dressing into the leaves and then divide among four bowls. Top with the watercress, hazelnuts, and half of an avocado per salad. Drizzle each with the remaining dressing. Sprinkle each with 1 Tbsp of the gomasio and a generous dusting of the magic powder. I like to tell my cooks the desired effect of the powder should look like a blackout. Serve immediately.

WATERMELON SALAD WITH TURMERIC-GINGER RELISH

Serves 2

This salad is so easy, so refreshing, so summer! The turmeric and ginger dressing also goes great with a celery and white bean salad or thinly sliced roasted squash with pine nuts or as a mignonette for oysters.

1 in [2.5 cm] piece ginger
3 in [7.5 cm] piece fresh turmeric
1 recipe Big Flavor Dressing (page 48)
1 tsp fresh coarsely ground black pepper
1 lb [455 g] chilled watermelon

Peel and thinly slice the ginger and turmeric crosswise to break down the long fibers that run the length of them. Transfer to a food processor and process until they're finely chopped, or mince or grate the turmeric and ginger on a Microplane. Transfer the minced turmeric and ginger to a bowl and add enough of the dressing to cover. Allow to marinate for 10 minutes. Stir in the black pepper. The relish holds up in the refrigerator for 1 week.

Cut the cold watermelon into two-bite pieces and top with the turmeric-ginger relish. Serve immediately.

CUCUMBER, PLUM, AND RICOTTA WITH CITRONETTE

Serves 2 to 4

I love incorporating stone fruit—especially plums with their bright, tart flavor—into salads. Start thinking of plums as your new tomato. In this recipe, the cucumbers provide a crisp and fresh note, while ricotta adds a nice richness.

2 cups [160 g] cucumber, sliced on the bias

1 Tbsp lemon juice or light vinegar, such as apple cider or champagne

½ cup [120 g] ricotta

2 cups [160 g] halved or quartered plums

¼ cup [60 ml] Citronette (page 45)

2 Tbsp roasted pine nuts (see page 105)

Flaky sea salt, for serving

In a small bowl, add the cucumber slices and lemon juice and toss. Let sit for a couple minutes to absorb the acid.

Spread the ricotta on a platter or large plate. Arrange the cucumbers and plums on top and drizzle with the citronette. Sprinkle with the pine nuts and flaky sea salt. Serve immediately.

CUCUMBER AND APRICOT SALAD WITH ALMOND MILK VINAIGRETTE

Serves 2 to 4

With crisp, cold cucumbers, soft, sweet fruit, and a delicate almond dressing, this dish is an ode to summer.

If it grows together, it goes together; melons are a delicious substitute for the apricots in this recipe.

2 cups [160 g] cucumber, sliced on the bias
2 Tbsp lemon juice or rice vinegar
2 cups [160 g] halved apricots
½ cup [120 ml] Almond Milk Vinaigrette (page 48)
2 to 3 Tbsp extra-virgin olive oil
10 whole basil leaves
Flaky sea salt

In a small bowl, add the cucumber slices and lemon juice and toss. Let sit for a couple minutes to absorb the acid.

In a large, shallow serving bowl, arrange the lemony cucumbers and apricots. Drizzle the dressing and olive oil over the top, dot with the whole basil leaves, and sprinkle with flaky sea salt. Serve immediately.

COLLARD GREEN AND PEACH SUMMER SALAD

Serves 2

My journey to avoid overusing trendy ingredients like kale continues. Enter collard greens: We're used to seeing them cooked, but I think they're just as wonderful raw. They start coming around the market during the time that ripe, juicy peaches make an appearance, so it should be no surprise that they pair perfectly together. I've added roasted parsnips and steamed soft cauliflower to this summer market salad blueprint, but I encourage you to play around with your other market finds and discover the combo that's right for you.

2 parsnips, scrubbed and sliced crosswise ⅛ in [3 mm] thick

½ tsp agave, honey, or maple syrup

2 Tbsp neutral oil, such as sunflower, grapeseed, safflower, or rice bran

Pinch kosher salt

Pinch chili powder

1 cup [100 g] cauliflower florets

½ cup [90 g] sprouted farro or other grain (see page 178)

4 collard or kale leaves, deribbed and cut into bite-size pieces

2 Tbsp extra-virgin olive oil

¼ cup [60 ml] Citronette (page 45)

1 ripe juicy peach, pitted and cut into bite-size pieces

2 Tbsp Dried Red Berry and Beet Pickle, using goji berries (page 77)

3 Tbsp roasted pecans (see page 105)

Preheat the oven to 400°F [200°C].

On a rimmed baking sheet, toss the parsnips with the agave and neutral oil and season with salt and chili powder. Roast, turning once, until the parsnips are tender, about 20 minutes. Let cool.

Fill a medium pot with salted water and place over medium-high heat. Add the cauliflower and cook until soft, about 10 minutes. Remove the cauliflower and add the farro to the pot. Bring to a boil and cook like

cont'd

pasta, until tender, about 10 minutes. Remove the pot from the heat and drain. Let the cauliflower and grains cool.

In a large bowl, add the collards and massage them with the olive oil. Let sit for a few minutes to tenderize.

Add the cooked and cooled cauliflower, farro, and parsnips to the collards. Add the citronette and toss to coat. Divide the salad between two plates and stud with the peach, pickle, and pecans. Serve immediately.

SHAVED MUSHROOM, DANDELION, AND PETAL SALAD

Serves 2

I like making this salad with fresh flowers during the summertime. The dandelion is very bitter and the petals have a subtle bite, giving the dish an interesting vegetal note. I also love the density of shaved raw mushrooms, and the adaptogenic powder brings in the umami. When plating, I like to layer each ingredient very intentionally, dressing each layer liberally, as mushrooms like to absorb the dressing.

Handful dandelion greens, cut into 2 in [5 cm] pieces

½ cup [120 ml] Citronette (page 45)

6 button-style mushrooms, sliced

¼ cup Roasted Nut Master Recipe made with walnuts (page 105)

¼ cup [8 g] shaved Parmesan cheese (optional)

2 Tbsp Super-Powered Powder (page 114)

Flaky sea salt

Edible flowers

Layer the dandelion greens on a platter or two plates, dressing with a bit of the citronette. Top with mushrooms, dressing with more citronette. Finish with one final drizzle of citronette; sprinkle on the walnuts, Parmesan (if using), powder, and flaky sea salt; and top with the edible flowers. Serve immediately.

WILD GREEN SALAD WITH PEA SHOOT PESTO AND AGED PECORINO

Serves 1 or 2

This wonderfully green, wild savory salad is another one of my favorites because the pea shoot pesto adds a lot of umami. You can find fresh watercress, chickweed, and purslane at the market in the spring and summer. Try to find wild foraged greens, rather than farmed varieties, so you can taste the richer, verdant flavor. But if you're making this another time of year or if you're unable to find any, arugula is an excellent substitute.

2 cups [40 g] tender wild greens

3 Tbsp Pea Shoot Pesto (page 63)

¼ cup [20 g] shaved aged pecorino, Parmesan, or Grana Padano cheese

In a large bowl, toss the greens, pesto, and cheese until well combined and serve immediately.

CHILLED NOODLES WITH PEANUT-GINGER SAUCE

Serves 2 to 4

I associate this recipe with New York Chinese takeout. I love dishes that are meant to be served at room temperature; they travel well and don't require a lot of fussing.

12 oz [360 g] Asian-style noodles, such as lo mein, ramen, or soba

1 bunch whole scallions, thinly sliced

1 recipe Peanut-Ginger Sauce (page 55)

2 tsp sesame oil

¼ cup [35 g] chopped peanuts or 2 Tbsp toasted sesame seeds

Fresh herbs, protein, or an assortment of crunchy vegetables (optional), for serving

Cook the noodles according to the package instructions. Rinse under cool water and drain well.

Transfer the noodles to a medium bowl and mix in the scallions and dressing. To serve, drizzle with the sesame oil and top with the peanuts. Make it a meal by adding lots of fresh herbs, a protein, and crunchy vegetables (if using). Leftovers can be stored in an airtight container in the refrigerator for 2 days.

SMOKED FISH SALAD WITH DAIKON, ASIAN PEAR, AND POPPY SEEDS

Serves 1 or 2

I learned this recipe from one of my favorite chefs, and it's super easy to make. You get a smoked fish, shred it, then let it sit in very flavorful vinegar to soak up all the bright flavors. It's refreshing, bold, and smoky. The daikon and Asian pear add a delightful finishing crunch.

½ cup [70 g] peeled and julienned daikon

½ cup [70 g] peeled and julienned Asian pear

¼ cup [60 ml] Big Flavor Dressing (page 48)

4 oz [115 g] smoked white fish

1 Tbsp poppy seeds or sesame seeds or ¼ cup [35 g] chopped peanuts

1 Tbsp sesame oil

In a large bowl, add the daikon and Asian pear, then the dressing, and toss to coat. Flake the smoked fish, removing any bones, and add to the bowl along with the seeds; gently fold in. Drizzle with the sesame oil, transfer to one or two plates, and serve.

POTATOES AND TOMATOES WITH TONNATO

Serves 2 to 4

Tonnato is an old-world sauce that's become more ubiquitous (and trendy) in the last few years. Made of poached fish and mayonnaise blended together to create a rich, multidimensional sauce, it's usually served with thinly sliced, cold veal. At Navy, I used to fry up gnocchi and serve it with this sauce. But I just love potato salad and tomatoes in the summertime, so instead of using a simple aioli in this dish, I use up any leftover fish I have and dress my salad in an unctuous tonnato. Adding thinly sliced sushi-grade raw tuna in place of the potatoes is a lux upgrade to this salad.

1 lb [455 g] potatoes, peeled and chopped

½ cup [120 g] Tonnato (page 60) or Green Olive or Caper Aioli (page 58)

¼ cup [60 ml] extra-virgin olive oil

Flaky sea salt

1 lb [455 g] tomatoes, cut into chunky irregular diamond cuts or thick slices

Fill a large pot with salted water and place over medium-high heat. Add the potatoes and cook until very tender, about 20 minutes. Be aggressive when straining them. This will rough them up, creating dents and grooves to which the tonnato and tomato juices can adhere. Let cool.

Spread the tonnato on a large serving platter. Top with the cooled potatoes, drizzle with half of the extra-virgin olive oil, and sprinkle on some flaky sea salt. Arrange the cut tomatoes on top of the potatoes and sauce, drizzle with the remaining extra-virgin olive oil, and sprinkle with more flaky sea salt to finish. Serve immediately.

VEGETABLES

Small vegetable-forward dishes are what I am known for, and it is my favorite way of honoring and showcasing these nutrient-dense, vitamin-rich foods. Because vegetables are the key to our health, spending money on quality produce, preparing it simply, and serving with beautiful oil and crunchy salt or a garlicky aioli is something I can always get behind. Full of flavor and with so much to play with, these dishes in which vegetables are the star are the ones I have the most fun developing, so consider this section your go-to guide for veggie flexing.

THE FORGOTTEN VEGETABLES

Why do some vegetables get more love than others? All vegetables are good vegetables! Working as a chef at several downtown bootstrap restaurants, I worked with both expensive and inexpensive vegetables to stay on budget. But the exercise of creating dishes out of lesser known or "forgotten" vegetables led me to so much creativity in the kitchen. Here are a few veggies to explore when you're feeling stuck in a greens rut.

Celery was actually very common back in the early 1900s. Almost all menus from that era had a celery dish, whether served as a crudité with radish and olives or poached in a cream. It has mostly fallen out of favor for the last hundred years, but I don't know why—it has such a crunch and acidic deliciousness. I like to use it in a mignonette for oysters, as a salad piled on uni toast, or in main or side course salads, such as a salad of celery, radish, Parmesan, parsley, and anchovy dressing, or one with celery, boquerones (white briny anchovies), parsley, and Marcona almonds.

Jicama is a bit of an ugly vegetable, but it is the crunchiest of all the crunchy vegetables. It's got a bit of starchiness to it that's also very pleasing, similar to the starchiness of peak raw summer corn or underripe apples. I like to combine it with Asian pear, as they are similar in texture but have contrasting flavors. Try cutting it into thin rounds for an easy snack or using as a shredded slaw base with a sesame vinaigrette.

Kohlrabi is a crunchy, bulbous vegetable that lends itself perfectly to crudités—it has a subtle flavor everyone will like and goes well with any dip you pair it up with. Consider adding it to any and all crunchy salads in your repertoire; I personally like it combined with apple, walnut, and Parmesan.

Plantains are tropical, starchy fruits related to bananas. They are universal and diverse and can be boiled, baked, fried, steamed, or grilled. Grated, they can be formed into balls for a tacky and tasty dumpling or used along with or in place of masa for tamales. Used green or so ripe they're almost black, they can be sliced and fried or even steamed whole for a tasty side.

Rutabaga, a large root vegetable that's a cross between a turnip and a cabbage, has a purple and orange exterior with a bright orange interior. Use as you would a winter squash or sweet potato.

Parsnips are carrots' fancier cousins. They have the sweet and savory complexity of a carrot with a touch of anise. But unlike carrots, parsnips are not very good raw. I enjoy them best cut into coins and roasted or made into a mash.

Beet greens, as the name suggests, are the leaves that grow on beets, and they have the most iron of all the leafy greens. They have a mild, sweet, and earthy flavor that's incredibly craveable, and they're most delicious cooked up slow and low with lots of good extra-virgin olive oil.

SALT-BAKED VEGETABLES WITH CACAO SEED MIX

Serves 6

I love a pièce de résistance at a dinner party, and this dish is just that. It comes to the table encased in a pyramid-like salt crust. When it's cracked open in front of everyone, everything rolls out, and people can pick their vegetable. The cacao is an umami bomb, adding an intellectual kind of flavor. This dish is a great way to celebrate the season's best vegetables from the dedicated hard workers of your favorite farm.

2 egg whites or ¼ cup [25 g] flaxseed meal mixed with 1 cup [240 ml] filtered water

3 lb [1.4 kg] kosher salt (use the inexpensive stuff)

4 to 8 large banana or plantain leaves, large cabbage leaves, or rehydrated lotus leaves

2 lb [910 g] of the market's in-season star vegetables, such as carrots, cabbage, beets, potato, or winter or summer squash, cut as needed to stack

½ cup [120 ml] super high-quality olive oil or sesame oil (splurge)

¼ cup [25 g] Toasted Cacao Nib, Buckwheat, and Sesame Mix (page 108) or another seed or nut blend

Salsa Verde (page 64), and Ginger-Garlic Mojo (page 50) for serving (optional)

Preheat the oven to 350°F [180°C]. Remove the top rack, leaving only one rack in the oven's lowest position.

In a bowl, whip the egg whites. If using flax meal, let the flax and water sit for 5 minutes and then whip until stiff. Add the kosher salt and the whipped egg whites and mix to combine. If the mixture is too dry, add 1 to 2 Tbsp water.

On a rimmed baking sheet, spread out 1 cup [200 g] of the salt mixture, pat it down, and lay a large leaf on top. Stack your vegetables, using large skewers if needed to hold your stack together. Wrap the bottom leaf up and around the stack and use the remaining leaves to fully wrap the vegetables (remove skewers!). Secure the top with twine, if needed. The leaves protect the vegetables from getting too salty. Form the remaining salt mixture around the wrapped vegetables, encasing them fully. Bake for 1 hour.

Crack the crust open in front of your guests. Serve with the oil, seed mix, and salsa and mojo (if using) so guests can help themselves.

NOODLE BOWL WITH CARROTS AND FRESH HERBS

Serves 2

There is no limit to the amount of fresh herbs you use in this dish. Along with a bright plum sauce and crunchy vegetables, this divine and simple noodle bowl is a favorite meal during the spring and summer months because it is cool and super refreshing.

SAVORY PLUM SAUCE

1 Tbsp ground mustard

1 in [2.5 cm] piece ginger, minced or grated

1 garlic clove, minced or grated

2 Tbsp Worcestershire sauce

½ cup [150 g] fruit conserve like Plum Molasses (page 100) or Cranberry-Hibiscus Molasses (page 100)

¼ cup [65 g] ketchup

2 Tbsp soy sauce

1 Tbsp tamarind paste (optional)

BOWL

4 oz [115 g] noodles, such as rice, buckwheat, soba, or kelp

1 or 2 green onions, thinly sliced

8 oz [230 g] shaved carrots or other vegetables, such as cabbage, radishes, romaine, chicories, fennel, or celery

¼ to ½ cup [10 to 20 g] roughly chopped herbs, such as cilantro or a mix of mint and basil

Sliced fresh chile, such as Thai bird or jalapeño, depending on your heat preference

2 Tbsp chopped peanuts or Summer Gomasio (page 106)

To make the plum sauce: In a small bowl, add the ground mustard, ginger, and garlic and pour the Worcestershire sauce over. Mix everything together and let sit for 5 minutes. Add the fruit conserve, ketchup, soy sauce, and tamarind paste (if using) and mix well.

To make the bowl: Bring a medium pot of salted water to a boil. Add the noodles and cook until al dente. Drain and rinse with cold water. Transfer to a medium bowl and toss with the plum sauce, green onions, and half of the shaved vegetables. Divide between two serving bowls and top each with the remaining vegetables, herbs, chile, and peanuts. Serve immediately.

CUBAN BEANS, COCONUT RICE, AND STEAMED SWEET PLANTAINS

Serves 4

This dish is my heritage on a plate, an homage to the Caribbean. You can substitute for the plantains with slow-roasted sweet potatoes coated with oil and seasoned with salt and a pinch of honey to create a sweet, tacky texture similar to the plantain.

CUBAN BEANS

¼ cup [60 ml] olive oil or neutral oil, such as sunflower, grapeseed, safflower, or rice bran

3 Tbsp Summer Sofrito, Recaito Any Other Time (page 92)

3 Tbsp tomato paste

3 Tbsp pimiento-stuffed olives with 2 Tbsp of their brine

2 cups [520 g] cooked black or pink beans in their broth, or ½ cup [90 g] cooked sprouted beans (see page 178)

1 Tbsp red-wine vinegar

COCONUT RICE

1½ cups [300 g] short- or long-grain white rice

2 Tbsp desiccated unsweetened coconut

1 cup [240 ml] coconut milk

Pinch salt

Aromatics, such as 2 slices ginger; 2 in [5 cm] piece lemongrass, smashed; 10 fresh curry leaves; or whole culantro leaf (optional)

4 ripe, almost-black plantains

Fermented Hot Sauce (page 80), for serving

Sliced avocado, for serving

To make the beans: In a medium pot over medium-high heat, add the oil and sofrito and allow them to warm up together. When they begin to sizzle slightly, add the tomato paste and fry until it darkens by a few shades. Add the olives and their brine. Stir to combine. Add the beans and their broth. Stir, then simmer, uncovered, over medium-low heat for 20 minutes. Once the flavors have developed, remove from the heat and stir in the vinegar. Set aside.

cont'd

To make the coconut rice: Rinse the rice under cold water until the water runs clear. Add the rice, coconut, coconut milk, salt, and aromatics, along with ¾ cup [180 ml] filtered water, to a medium, heavy pot or rice cooker. Bring to a simmer over medium heat. Decrease the heat to low, cover, and cook for 25 minutes until the grains are tender.

Cut off both ends of each plantain and make a lengthwise incision in the peel, keeping the peels intact; this allows them to expand while cooking. In a large pot, bring 6 cups [1.4 L] water to a boil. Add the plantains and simmer over medium heat for 20 minutes until tender. Leave the plantains in the pot with the water until ready to use. Be prepared to serve them right away, as they seize up when cooled too much.

Divide the rice among four bowls and top with the beans. Remove the plantains from the water, peel, and slice into coins or make one cut lengthwise. Place on top of the rice and beans. Serve with hot sauce and a slice of avocado.

GRILLED OR STEAMED TURNIPS AND THEIR GREENS WITH WALNUT-KIMCHI DIP

Serves 2

I love fresh steamed or grilled turnips because they have such a delicious, juicy bite. The walnut-kimchi dip is a nice complement to the subtle flavoring of the turnip. I like to use young turnips because they're on the smaller side, but if yours are larger, cut them in half before serving.

1 bunch young turnips or radishes, preferably with healthy greens attached

Extra-virgin olive oil

Sea salt

Walnut-Kimchi Dip (page 65), for serving

Rinse and separate the turnips and their greens.

IF GRILLING: Set the turnips or radishes on a clean grill or grill pan over medium heat and cook until tender and juicy, about 15 minutes, flipping them midway.

IF STEAMING: Place the turnips or radishes in a steaming basket set over a pot of boiling water, or boil in shallow, salted water until tender, 10 to 15 minutes.

Remove the turnips and replace with the greens. Grill or steam for 30 seconds until bright green.

Serve the turnips and greens on a platter drizzled with olive oil and sprinkled with sea salt, alongside the walnut-kimchi dip.

PLANTAIN DUMPLING STEW

Serves 2

This soup is my interpretation of a sancocho, a traditional Latin American stew. In this version, I use cooked plantains to make dense, tasty dumplings that absorb all the delicious, layered flavors in the broth.

¼ cup [60 ml] olive oil

3 Tbsp Summer Sofrito, Recaito Any Other Time (page 92)

2 Tbsp tomato paste

¼ cup [60 ml] white wine

4 cups [960 ml] Turmeric-Ginger-Chile Vegetable Broth (page 88)

1 green plantain

2 pinches salt

1 lb [455 g] root vegetables, such as carrots, russet potato, or yucca, peeled and cut into 2 in [5 cm] pieces

2 cups [30 g] shredded kale or collard greens

½ bunch cilantro, stems finely chopped, leaves coarsely chopped

Juice of 1 lime

In a medium soup pot over medium heat, add the oil and sofrito and fry for 4 minutes. Add the tomato paste and fry until it darkens by a few shades, 4 to 5 minutes. Add the wine and cook, stirring, until it is reduced by half, 2 to 3 minutes. Add the broth and bring to a simmer.

Meanwhile, peel the plantain and cut into 1 in [2.5 cm] chunks. Process the chunks in a food processor to a smooth paste, or grate with the fine side of a box grater. Season the plantain purée with the salt and roll into six to eight balls.

Once the soup is simmering, add the plantain dumplings and root vegetables and simmer for 30 minutes. Add the kale and simmer for 5 minutes more. Divide the stew between two bowls and serve, topped with a large handful of cilantro and a drizzle of lime juice.

SQUASH WITH PEANUT-COCONUT CURRY

Serves 2

This is a super nourishing and gratifying dish, especially on a cold evening. The preparation is incredibly easy, and the curry can be used as a soup, as a sauce served over rice or noodles, or as a lovely broth to poach fish.

1 medium squash, such as acorn, butternut, or koginut, peeled, if needed

2 Tbsp coconut oil

2 Tbsp Fresh Curry Paste (page 94)

1 Tbsp Spice Mix (page 117)

2 cups [480 ml] Coconut-Ginger Broth (page 87) or Turmeric-Ginger-Chile Vegetable Broth (page 88)

¼ cup [35 g] roasted peanuts (see page 105), chopped

1 tsp Chile Paste (page 94), or to taste

Spiced Finishing Oil (page 117) or extra-virgin olive oil, for serving

Lemon or lime juice or any kind of vinegar, for serving

Fill a pot big enough to fit the squash with water and bring to a boil over medium-high heat. Add the whole squash and boil until tender, 10 to 20 minutes depending on the type and size. Remove carefully and let cool. Halve, seed, and slice the squash and set aside.

In a large, shallow pot, warm the coconut oil, then add the curry paste and sauté for 2 minutes until fragrant. Add the spice mix and stir for 1 minute. Add the broth and simmer for 10 minutes until slightly reduced and the flavors have melded. Add the peanuts and chili paste, and simmer for 5 minutes longer.

Pour the sauce onto a shallow bowl or platter. Top with the sliced steamed squash. Finish with a drizzle of oil and a dash of acidity, and serve.

CHARRED WINTER SQUASH WITH SUMAC YOGURT AND PISTACHIO

Serves 2 to 4

This is a great, easy, end-of-autumn dish. Instead of roasting the squash, I like to boil it until al dente, then slice it and give it a quick little fry in a pan for more depth. The cooling sumac yogurt and nutty pistachio are lovely additions to the flavor profile of this dish. Consider finishing with a pickle or hot sauce too.

1 large winter squash, such as kabocha or koginut, peeled, if needed

Neutral oil, such as grapeseed or rice bran, for frying

1 cup [240 g] Fennel Pollen Yogurt (page 38), sumac variation

¼ cup [35 g] roasted pistachios (see page 105)

Bring a large pot of salted water to a simmer and add the whole squash. Simmer until tender, about 20 minutes. Remove carefully and let cool. Halve, seed, and cut into wedges. Add a thin film of oil to a pan over medium-high heat. Add the wedges and let char, untouched, for 5 minutes. Flip and repeat.

Spread the yogurt on a large plate and top with the warm squash. Finish with a sprinkle of the pistachios and serve.

CORN AND BLACK SESAME TAMALES

Makes 8 tamales

The yucca pasteles of Puerto Rico and other parts of the Caribbean were the inspiration for me starting to add a little yucca to my tamales. When paired with the polenta-style cornmeal, it makes for a rich, dense, moisture-filled bite.

1 lb [455 g] yucca

½ cup [120 ml] filtered water

2 ears corn, kernels grated off the cob (save cobs for future broth making)

½ cup [70 g] polenta-style cornmeal

1 tsp salt

1 Tbsp Summer Sofrito, Recaito Any Other Time (page 92) or other flavor paste, or 1 tsp minced garlic

1 Tbsp roasted black sesame seeds (see page 105)

Eight 10 by 5 in [25 by 12.5 cm] plantain or banana leaves or 8 fresh corn husks

Fermented Hot Sauce (page 80), for serving

Grate the yucca using a box grater or process in a food processor until it resembles a dough. Add the water, corn, cornmeal, salt, and sofrito and mix together or process for another minute. Fold in the sesame seeds and mix well to combine. Let sit for 15 minutes to thicken.

On a clean counter, lay out the plantain leaves or corn husks. Add ½ cup [200 g] of the mixture to each leaf or husk and fold in half. Grabbing the edges, make a 1 in [2.5 cm] fold downward until you have created a compact package. Fold each end inward and secure each package with twine. The tamales should be 2 by 5 in [5 by 12.5 cm].

Bring a large pot of salted water to a simmer, drop in the tamales, and cook for 40 minutes until the mixture is firm, making sure the water stays at a gentle simmer so the packets don't slosh around too much. Remove the packets from the water with tongs and set aside to cool. Open up the packets, remove the tamales, and serve with hot sauce. Tamales will keep in a lidded container in the refrigerator for 4 to 5 days or in the freezer for 6 months.

FRESH CORN POLENTA WITH CORN AND PARMESAN BROTH

Serves 2 to 4

This simple, nurturing dish is a great way to utilize all your leftover cobs and rinds. It makes a delicious broth, with the sweetness of the cob adding to the umami of the Parmesan and nutritional yeast.

4 cups [960 ml] Corn and Parmesan Broth (page 87)

½ cup [70 g] polenta, soaked in the broth overnight in the refrigerator if using coarsely ground

4 ears corn, kernels sliced off the cob (save cobs for future broth making)

¼ cup [15 g] nutritional yeast

¼ cup [15 g] grated Parmesan cheese, plus more for topping

Salt (optional)

Extra-virgin olive oil

Ground black pepper (optional)

In a medium pot over medium heat, whisk together the broth and polenta. Stir occasionally to prevent the polenta from sinking to the bottom and potentially sticking and burning. The more it thickens, the more frequently it should be stirred. After 20 minutes, stir continuously for an additional 5 to 10 minutes. Stir in the fresh corn kernels and nutritional yeast and cook for an additional 2 minutes. Stir in the Parmesan. Taste and season with salt if needed.

To serve, ladle into shallow bowls, drizzle with olive oil, and top with Parmesan and a couple turns of a pepper grinder (if using). Leftovers will keep in a lidded container in the refrigerator for 2 to 3 days.

CORN AND POTATO CHOWDER

Serves 2 to 4

This is one of the easiest dishes to make, especially if you already have some Corn and Parmesan Broth (page 87) stashed away in your freezer. My secret to turning it into a chowder is that I add a little bit of corn flour; it helps thicken the broth, and the beautiful speckles add a lovely visual element to the chowder.

2 Tbsp olive oil

2 leeks, thinly sliced and rinsed free of grit

Pinch salt

Pinch cayenne (optional)

1 Tbsp corn flour

¼ cup [60 ml] white wine

2 ears corn, kernels grated off the cob (save cobs for future broth making)

1 large russet potato, peeled and cubed

4 cups [960 ml] Corn and Parmesan Broth (page 87)

¼ cup [60 ml] heavy cream

In a medium soup pot over medium-low heat, add the olive oil, leeks, salt, and cayenne (if using) and cook until tender, about 10 minutes. Add the corn flour and mix well. Add the wine and simmer for 5 minutes. Add the corn, potato, and broth. Simmer for 10 minutes or until the potatoes are soft and tender. Add the cream and simmer for 5 minutes more. Taste, season with salt if necessary, and serve. Leftovers will keep in a lidded container in the refrigerator for 2 to 3 days.

GRAINS

Growing up, I had a creamy bowl of oats or cream of wheat in the mornings and rice with dinner every day. Grains are such a big part of our meals—they give us the energy to zip around and do what we need to do, and they feel like a hug when we are depleted. They provide fiber to cleanse our insides. If you think about how we use grains today, they are in everything that is delicious in the world, such as bread, pasta, and cake.

I try to seek out heritage grains when I can. While they may cost more, they have a delicious nutty flavor and build a foundation for better farming practices that, in turn, help save our planet and us from diseases. These grains have not been overproduced or stripped of nutrients, so it's vital to seek them out and incorporate them into your overall intake. While processed grains such as white rice and wheat for white bread are okay here and there, incorporating some whole grains into your regular rotation is key for a well-rounded diet.

ANATOMY
of a Dragon Bowl

A dragon bowl is a bowl by many names: *macrobiotic* or *macro bowl*, *Buddha bowl*, *grain bowl*, or *nourish bowl*. The term *dragon bowl* comes from the great New York City vegan restaurant Angelica Kitchen, where I cooked as a young chef on and off throughout the late 1990s. The restaurant named it for the decorative dragons on the outside of the bowls. The bowls were rather inexpensive and found in the Bowery, the restaurant district that also supplied the restaurants in neighboring Chinatown.

The foundation of the dragon bowl is based on the macrobiotic principles of cuisine: the importance of eating whole foods grown locally, eating foods in season, and eating clean, unprocessed food from which your body can most benefit. The truth is, you can make a dragon bowl out of anything as long as you have the following components:

Whole Grains

A source of fiber, nutrients, and energy.

- Brown rice
- Coconut rice
- Quinoa

Orange Vegetables

A source of beta-carotene and vitamin C.

- Steamed carrots
- Roasted kabocha squash
- Sweet potatoes

Green Vegetables

They provide nutrients, vitamins, and minerals. I like to think that green vegetables are like a life force because they reflect the green of the earth.

- Steamed kale
- Soft lettuces
- Sprouts (see page 178)
- Steamed greens in a Toasted Barley–Seaweed–Bonito Dashi (page 86)

Protein

Fuels our system and our cells.

- Beans
- Eggs
- Fish
- Steamed tofu

Sauce

For flavor, but also an excellent opportunity to inject the bowl with additional superfoods for maximum nutrients.

- Green Tahini (page 54)
- Sumac Yogurt (see page 38)
- Black Sesame–Chili Vinaigrette (page 44)
- Peanut-Ginger Sauce (page 55)

Seaweed

Lots of minerals and iodine.

- Hijiki
- Wakame
- Cucumber and Dulse Pickle (page 76)

Pickle

These are great for digestion, as are all fermented elements.

- Fermented cabbage and onion
- Dried Red Berry and Beet Pickle (page 77)
- Pickled Mustard Seed (page 78)
- Cucumber and Dulse Pickle (page 76)

These are just examples—what you can use is limitless. I like to utilize whatever I have in the refrigerator: Maybe I have some leftover steamed vegetables from the day before, so I can use that as a base for a quick and balanced meal, and then fill in the crucial elements of the bowl from there. I like to pair my dragon bowls with a brothy soup of some kind, such as a miso soup or a mineral broth. These elements together make for a very fulfilling, nutritionally balanced meal and align with the Buddhist philosophy of balance.

TIGER BOWL

Serves 2

At Café Henrie, I devised a concept where the entire menu was bowls, right before the grab-and-go bowl chains trend took off. This dish is my interpretation of the poke bowl.

4 oz [115 g] tuna or other sashimi-style raw fish, cut into ½ in [1.3 cm] cubes

½ cup [120 ml] Leche de Tigre (page 49)

¼ cup [60 ml] Beet–Sunflower Seed Sauce (page 53)

1 cup [200 g] cooked coconut rice (see page 212) or sticky rice

1 tsp Gomasio (page 105)

In a small bowl, toss the fish in the leche de tigre and let it sit for 5 minutes.

Swirl 2 Tbsp of the sunflower seed sauce in each bowl. Add the rice, top with the gomasio, and add the marinated fish with its sauce. Serve immediately.

DRESSED RICE WITH SHISO AND SUMMER GOMASIO

Serves 2

I love to dress a beautiful plate of rice with garnishes, whether I'm entertaining or cooking for myself. I might do a rice salad or an Indian-inspired dressed rice. This dish was inspired by one of my favorite Japanese restaurants in New York, Omen Azen, where they have simple, delicious shiso rice. Try topping it with avocado, roe, and/or pickled vegetables for added flair.

1 cup [200 g] Japanese short-grain rice

1¼ cups [300 ml] spring or filtered water

2 pinches salt

A few shakes of rice wine vinegar

20 shiso leaves

1 Tbsp light toasted sesame oil

2 Tbsp Summer Gomasio (page 106)

6 ume (pickled plums), pitted and finely minced

In a small, sturdy pot with a lid, rinse the rice by swirling it in water a few times with your hand. Drain and repeat three times (use the milky water to water your plants rather than discarding). Let the washed rice sit for 10 minutes.

Add the water and salt to the rice pot, cover, and simmer over medium-high heat for 5 minutes. Decrease the heat to medium-low and cook for 20 minutes. Remove from the heat. Swaddle the lid of the pot with a kitchen towel and place it back on the pot. Let the rice rest for 5 minutes.

Fluff the rice and transfer to a shallow ceramic serving bowl. Let sit for 5 minutes. With your thumb, cover the top of the rice wine vinegar bottle and shake over the rice, gently raining about 20 drops over the top.

Stack the shiso leaves, reserving a couple of leaves for garnish. Cut them lengthwise into super thin strips, gather the strips, and mince them finely. You can run a knife through them a few more times to get them super minced. Do this right before serving the rice so the shiso stays fresh and vibrant green. Fold the minced shiso into the rice.

To finish, drizzle with the sesame oil, sprinkle with the gomasio, and dot with the minced ume and reserved shiso. Serve immediately.

SPROUTED WHOLE GRAINS WITH BROCCOLI PESTO

Serves 2

I love cooking broccoli until it's really tender and serving it almost like a salad, or in this case, a pesto dish. It's another quick plate that's perfect for a last-minute meal or quick side.

1 cup [200 g] chopped broccoli, steamed or char-grilled

1 cup [200 g] cooked sprouted grains (see page 178) or leftover brown rice or cooked pasta

¾ cup [180 g] Broccoli Pesto (page 65)

Extra-virgin olive oil

In a medium bowl, toss together the broccoli, grains, and pesto. Serve with a heavy-handed drizzle of extra-virgin olive oil.

TURMERIC LENTIL RICE WITH MUSTARD AND CUMIN SEEDS

Serves 4

Serving rice at a dinner party might not seem fun, but if you dress the rice right, you can create an intentional, layered, visually appealing dish full of different textures and flavors for sharing. Chickpeas are also delicious here.

1½ cups [290 g] basmati rice

½ cup [80 g] sprouted lentils (see page 178)

2 tsp whole mustard seed

½ tsp whole cumin seed

1 tsp dried ground turmeric

1 tsp salt

1 tsp Chile Paste (page 94, optional)

1 tsp preserved lemon purée

1½ cups [360 ml] broth or filtered water

1 Tbsp coconut oil, ghee, or any oil

1 recipe Carrot Harissa (page 95)

½ cup [120 g] Greek-style yogurt, strained

¼ cup [27 g] Turmeric-Chili Almonds (page 109)

¼ cup [10 g] chopped cilantro

IF USING A RICE COOKER: Add the rice, lentils, mustard seed, cumin seed, turmeric, salt, chile paste (if using), preserved lemon, broth, and coconut oil and press the start button.

IF USING THE STOVE TOP: Add the rice, lentils, mustard seed, cumin seed, turmeric, salt, chile paste (if using), preserved lemon, broth, and coconut oil to a medium, heavy pot and place over medium heat. Bring to a simmer, cover, decrease the heat to low, and cook for 25 minutes.

While the rice is cooking, in a small bowl, stir together the harissa and yogurt.

Transfer the rice to a serving bowl and top with the almonds and lots of fresh chopped cilantro. Serve with harissa yogurt on the side.

SEAFOOD

While I indulge in meat from time to time, I identify as pescatarian. I've always thought the people who look the healthiest are the pescatarians, and most are profoundly connected to food.

Fish is the most delicate item to cook, in my opinion. It has a very small window from the time it's raw to overcooked and dry. However, when prepared just right, fish is succulent, more so than any other food.

Learning to perfectly cook a fish is a skill we should all strive for, and it is a talent I want to help you develop. First, the fish must be super fresh and not frozen—frozen fish is best only in moist applications like stews and soups. I'm not as into hard-cooking (pan-fried, deep-fried, grilled, or broiled) fish because it floods your kitchen with vapor that sits and smells rancid and almost always cooks out the moisture and albumen, making the fish dry. Soft-cooking fish (steaming or baking in a low-temperature oven at home) is my ideal method. Your kitchen does not suffer, and you'll most likely achieve better results because the cooking window is slightly longer and thus more forgiving.

ANATOMY

of a Crudo

A delicious crudo with lots of lime is one of my favorite meals. I especially love crudos because they are so delicately beautiful while being so simple to make: You slice your fish and plate the dish. The most crucial detail for a perfect crudo is making sure to use only local and incredibly fresh fish. I sometimes like to get a whole fish and break it down because, ideally, the freshest fish hasn't been opened and exposed to bacteria yet.

Serving crudos to friends and loved ones is so satisfying. You can never go wrong with a fresh and light offering, especially during the hot summer months. For the most part, I serve my fish fresh with a quick dressing drizzled over it, but you can also cure the fish with salt, a salt and sugar mix, a seaweed process, or lemon juice.

There are four elements for a perfect crudo: the fish, something acidic, something crunchy, and something fatty.

Fish

Always go with the freshest and most local fish, or sushi grade. Select fish that isn't too fibrous, and always keep it really cold to keep bacteria at bay and make it easier to slice. Feel free to play around with different cuts: a slice that looks like sashimi, a smaller dice like ceviche, or bigger chunks like poke.

Salmon

Arctic char

Ahi or tuna

Black or striped bass

Porgy

Acid

My top acid to use is lime juice, but I also use lemon juice, vinegars, or a light vinaigrette. These give your crudo a pop of flavor and help with the curing process.

Lemon, lime, grapefruit, or yuzu juice

Rice vinegar, white wine vinegar, or apple cider vinegar

Citronette (page 45) or Black Sesame-Chili Vinaigrette (page 44)

cont'd

Crunch

There are so many ways to add a nice, satisfying crunch to your crudo. You want to balance the softness of the fish by having something to contrast it, so try crunchy vegetables or nuts.

- Sliced onion, fennel, cucumber, or celery, and nuts
- Sunflower, sesame, or poppy seeds
- Slivered almonds or toasted pine nuts

Fat

Fats add more depth to the dish and provide richness and another flavor element.

- Olive, sesame, or avocado oil
- Plain or strained yogurt
- Beet-Dill Yogurt (page 36) or Tahini Yogurt (page 36)
- Avocado
- Kombu Oil (page 119)

Finish

Don't forget to season crudo liberally with salt, fresh herbs, or even a bit of chile or tamari.

- Pine nuts, pickled dried fruit
- Cucumbers and magic powder
- Nori pesto
- Poppy seeds and Almond Milk Vinaigrette (page 48)
- Tonnato (page 60)
- Chile Paste (page 94)
- Pickled okra seeds made with Pickling Solution Master Recipe (page 76) and caviar

KOMBU-CURED FISH WITH QUINOA-POTATO CRISP

Serves 4

This is a favorite recipe from my days at Navy. Quinoa is super versatile, and I love the visual and textural element that it adds to this dish. The quinoa crisp provides a nice foundation for the cured fish in this recipe, but it also goes great with eggs and bacon in the morning.

2 lb [910 g] russet potatoes

½ cup [60 g] cooked red quinoa

1 tsp salt

1 lb [455 g] whole fluke fillet

1 recipe Kombu Cure (page 83)

¼ cup [60 g] strained yogurt

¼ cup [50 g] wasabi roe, or other fish roe

Neutral oil, such as sunflower, grapeseed, safflower, or rice bran, for frying

Preheat the oven to 350°F [180°C]. Line a 6 by 9 in [15 by 23 cm] pan with parchment paper and grease the paper well.

Peel and grate the potatoes directly into a medium bowl of water. Swish the potato around to remove some of the starch and let it sit for a couple of minutes. Drain and squeeze out excess water with your hands. The potato can also be put in a clean dish rag and twisted to release the remaining moisture. The drier they are, the easier they'll be to work with.

Transfer the potatoes to a bowl with the cooked quinoa. Add the salt and mix to combine. Transfer the potato mixture to the prepared sheet pan. Top with another piece of parchment and another sheet pan of the same size, right side up so it nests into the other. Weight down with a heavy heatproof item, such as a cast-iron lid or rock.

Bake for 30 minutes.

Meanwhile, cure the fluke using the kombu cure, following the instructions on page 83. Chill in the refrigerator for 2 hours or up to overnight.

After 30 minutes, remove the potato-quinoa mixture from the oven, remove the top sheet pan and weight, and set on a rack to cool completely. Chill in the refrigerator for at least 2 hours, or up to overnight.

Slice the fluke thinly and cut the potato-quinoa mixture into eight even pieces. In a small bowl, mix together the yogurt and roe.

Heat 1 in [2.5 cm] oil in a skillet over medium heat, add the potato-quinoa pieces, and fry until golden brown on both sides, 2 to 3 minutes per side. Fry in batches as needed. Transfer to a rack or paper towel–lined plate to drain.

To serve, add a swoosh of the roe yogurt, place the potato quinoa crisp on top, and finish with slices of the cured fluke.

GRILLED SQUID, GREEN TAHINI, AND CHILE VINEGAR

Serves 2

This dish is simple and quick enough for a weeknight meal, but showy enough to serve at a dinner party. It has an interesting pairing of herbs, seafood, and creamy tahini sauce, with a nice splash of chile vinegar for zippiness. Sometimes I swap out the squid for other seafood, like rock shrimp. It's nice on its own as an appetizer with good crusty bread to sop up all the sauciness, but it's also great served alongside a potato or grain salad as a main.

1 fresh Thai bird chile or ½ serrano or jalapeño pepper, seeded and thinly sliced

3 Tbsp white wine vinegar, cider vinegar, or rice vinegar

Salt

1 cup [20 g] arugula or baby greens

½ cup [10 g] mixed soft herbs, such as parsley, chervil, cilantro, and mint

1 green onion, sliced

8 oz [230 g] whole squid bodies, rinsed and dried

1 recipe Green Tahini (page 54), made with arugula

In a medium bowl, mix together the chile, vinegar, and a pinch of salt and let cure for 10 minutes. Set aside.

In a small bowl, mix together the arugula, herbs, and green onion. Set aside.

Season the squid well with salt. Using a charcoal grill, a dry griddle, or a cast-iron pan over high heat, cook the squid for 2 minutes on each side. Transfer the squid to a cutting board. Let it cool slightly, and then thinly slice. Immediately add the cut squid to the chile-vinegar dressing. Add the herb mixture to the squid and vinegar. Toss.

To serve, dollop the green tahini on a serving platter or large shallow bowl and scoop the squid mixture on top.

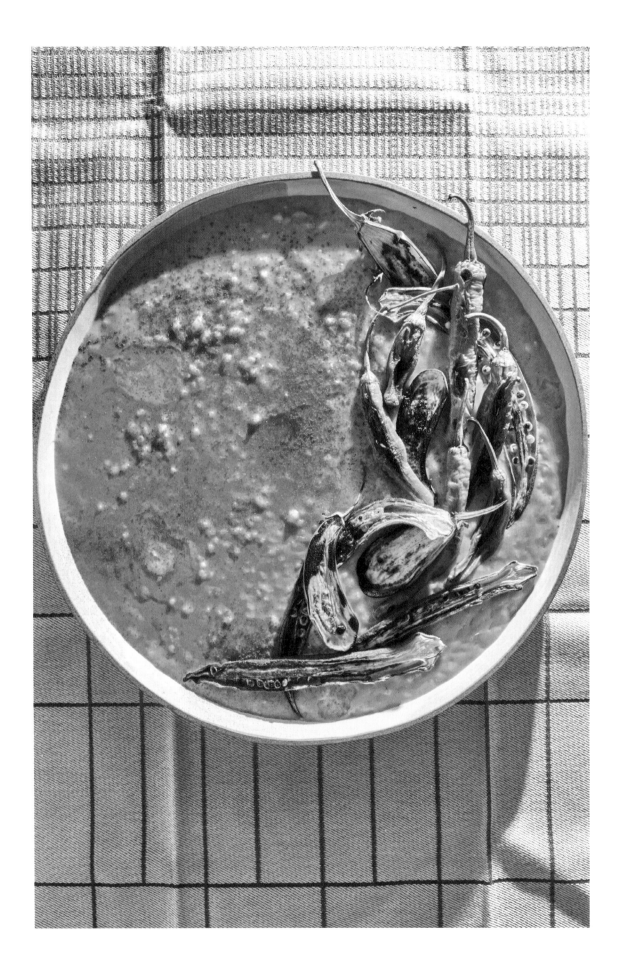

CLAMS AND BROTHY RICE

Serves 2 to 4

This is an effortless dish. The hack to making it super umami-rich
is adding romesco sauce to finish it, which helps thicken it and
give it big flavor.

1 lb [455 g] fresh clams

3 Tbsp olive oil

2 shallots, finely minced

Pinch salt

¼ cup [60 ml] white wine

3 Tbsp [45 g] unsalted butter

1 cup [200 g] short-grain rice

3 cups [720 ml] Stock Master Recipe (page 86)

¼ cup [60 g] Romesco Sauce (page 55)

Extra-virgin olive oil, for serving

Two hours before using the clams, cover them with filtered water
and let sit.

In a skillet or sauté pan over low heat, add the oil, half of the shallots,
and salt. Sweat until tender but without browning, about 10 minutes.
Increase the heat to medium, add the wine, and simmer until reduced
by half, 3 to 4 minutes. Remove the clams from the water (being careful
not to transfer any of the sediment), add them to the pan, and cover
with a lid. Cook until the clams have opened, 5 to 10 minutes, then
transfer them to a bowl along with their juices (clam liquor). Set aside.
Discard any clams that fail to open.

To the same pan over low heat, add the butter and remaining half of
the shallots and let sweat until tender but without browning, about
10 minutes. Add the rice and stir for 2 minutes, making sure all the rice
is coated in the butter and shallot. Slowly stir in only ¼ cup [60 ml] of
the broth, stirring the grains continuously to expel the starches from the
rice and thicken the broth. Add the remaining broth a ladle at a time,
stirring until the rice absorbs it before adding another ladle. When the
rice is tender and the broth is soupy and warm, turn off the heat and stir
in the romesco.

Divide the rice among two to four bowls, top with the clams and their
liquor, drizzle with high-quality olive oil, and serve.

POACHED PRAWNS IN MUSTARD SEED BUTTER SAUCE

Serves 2 to 4

Poaching is a super traditional way of cooking fish, but here I give it a twist by adding a bit of pickled mustard seed to heighten the flavor and provide a visual element. For garnish, I like to use wakame for both flavor and texture.

8 oz [230 g] large prawns, peeled, tails removed, and deveined
Salt
1 recipe Classic Butter Sauce (page 69)
2 Tbsp Pickled Mustard Seed (page 78)
Wakame or dulse, for garnish

Season the prawns with salt and set aside.

In a large pot, warm the butter sauce over low heat and stir in the pickled mustard seed. Submerge the prawns in the liquid and poach for 7 minutes, making sure not to let the sauce come to a boil or it will break. Remove the prawns, divide among plates, and serve with a drizzle of the butter sauce and a sprinkling of seaweed on top.

OLIVE OIL–POACHED SWORDFISH WITH CUCUMBER AND SPROUTED RYE BERRY YOGURT

Serves 2

One of my favorite ways of cooking fish, especially leaner ones like swordfish, is to poach it slowly in olive oil. Doing so allows the fish to retain its moisture, which makes it super succulent. I'm also a big fan of salty yogurt with fish—the sprouted grains in this one are traditional in Scandinavian cuisine, and I love the pop that their texture provides to the silky sauce.

8 oz [230 g] swordfish, rinsed and dried, cut into 2 thin pieces
Salt
1 cucumber, thinly sliced
1 Tbsp fresh lemon juice or cider or white wine vinegar
½ cup [120 ml] extra-virgin olive oil
Sprouted Rye Berry Yogurt (page 38)

Season the swordfish with 2 pinches of salt and set aside at room temperature to temper.

In a small bowl, toss the cucumber slices with the lemon juice and a pinch of salt.

In a shallow pan over low heat, warm the olive oil to 150°F [65°C]. Submerge the fish in the oil and poach for 4 minutes.

Smear two plates with the yogurt. Transfer the poached fish slices to the plates, reserving the flavorful strained oil for a future use if desired. Garnish the fish with the cucumber salad and drizzle with some of the poaching liquid to finish. Serve immediately.

PAPRIKA BROTH—POACHED STRIPED BASS WITH GRIBICHE

Serves 2

The paprika broth in this recipe has a rich, smoky, dense flavor profile that helps turn a basic fish into a very pleasing, simple dish.

Two 5 oz [140 g] pieces striped bass or other flaky white fish, rinsed and dried

2 pinches salt

1 Tbsp smoked paprika

2 cups [480 ml] Stock Master Recipe (page 86) or other flavorful broth

4 oz [115 g] baby potatoes, peeled and uniformly chopped

¼ white onion or 3 green onions, thinly sliced

Gribiche (page 59), for serving

Season the fish with the salt and set aside at room temperature to temper.

In a small, dry pot big enough to hold both fish fillets, toast the paprika over medium heat, stirring constantly, until very fragrant but not burnt, about 3 minutes. Add the stock and potatoes, bring to a gentle boil, and cover. Cook until the potatoes are tender, about 15 minutes, then add the fish, cover again, turn off the heat, and let poach for 5 minutes.

Divide the fish and broth between two bowls and serve topped with the onion and a helping of gribiche on the side.

SALT AND PEPPER SEAFOOD FRY

Serves 2 to 4

The fermented black beans that I use in my Black Pepper Umami Powder have such a wonderful funky aroma that I love, and that works well in savory or sweet applications. This tempura batter recipe is a great one to have in your repertoire—try it with other fish, vegetables, or even fruit.

1 cup [140 g] all-purpose flour

½ tsp salt

½ cup [70 g] cornmeal or corn masa

¼ cup [35 g] rice starch, potato starch, or cornstarch

1 tsp baking powder

2 cups [480 ml] water

1 egg, separated

Neutral oil, such as sunflower, grapeseed, safflower, or rice bran, for frying

8 oz [230 g] market's freshest fish, such as cod, squid, or rock shrimp, cut into bite-size pieces

2 Tbsp Black Pepper Umami Powder (page 114)

Fresh lemon juice or vinegar, for sprinkling

Mayonnaise (page 58) or Green Olive Aioli (page 58), for serving

Set up a medium dredge bowl with ½ cup [70 g] flour and ¼ tsp salt.

In a large bowl, mix the remaining ½ cup [70 g] of the all-purpose flour, the cornmeal, starch, baking powder, and the remaining ¼ tsp salt. Make a well in the center. Add the water and egg yolk. Slowly mix everything together to make a batter and set aside.

In a small bowl, whip the egg white until stiff peaks form, fold the egg whites into the batter, and set aside.

Add the oil to a sturdy medium pot to a depth of 3 in [7.5 cm]. Warm slowly to 375°F [190°C].

Dredge the seafood in the flour, then dip in the batter. Working with four pieces at a time in order not to crowd the pot, add the seafood to the hot oil and fry until golden on all sides, about 5 minutes. Remove from the oil, drain over an oven rack or sheet pan lined with a paper towel, and dust with the umami powder while still piping hot.

Sprinkle with lemon juice and serve with the mayonnaise.

FISH EN CROÛTE

Serves 2 to 4

Another favorite from my restaurant Navy, fish en croûte is classic in its flare and showy in the best way. But I promise this visually stunning dish will surprise you with how straightforward it is to make.

Two 4 by 6 in [10 by 15 cm] sheets frozen puff pastry, preferably all-butter, thawed

2 whole trout or another firm, thin fish, cleaned, deboned, and all fins removed, or 2 large fillets of black bass or other firm fish

½ tsp salt

3 Tbsp [45 g] heavy cream or whole or alternative milk

1 cup [240 g] Herby Sorrel Yogurt (page 37)

Preheat the oven to 425°F [220°C]. Line a baking sheet with parchment paper.

Place the chilled puff pastry on a cutting board. Place the fish on the puff pastry. With a sharp knife, cut around the shape of the fish, leaving a ¼ in [6 mm] border. Remove the fish and score the pastry by making a slight incision without cutting through the dough to give it a decorative element.

Season the fish and the cavities with the salt. Place on the prepared baking sheet, top with the pastry dough, and brush the dough with the beaten egg. Let chill for 5 minutes in the refrigerator or freezer.

Bake until golden brown, about 15 minutes.

To serve, spoon the yogurt on a serving platter and top with the fish.

PERFECT STEAMED FISH

A steamed fish dish is the easiest to make, needing only three steps from start to finish. It's also my preferred way of cooking fish in a small New York City apartment, as this gentle process is less smelly than when you cook fish using a hard, fast fry. After removing the whole fish from the refrigerator, allow it to come to room temperature for 15 minutes. If it's too cold, it won't cook as evenly. I sometimes like to marinate the whole fish before steaming it to inject some extra flavor, so if you have the time, marinate it with wine, mirin, or soy sauce—whatever you have on hand.

Ultimately, I want to push you to understand what a fish feels like from raw to done. Steaming might not be the best technique for that, but it's a good way to begin honing your cooking instincts. When you're pan-frying fish, it's easier to tell when it's done. But when you are steaming it, you don't want to keep uncovering the pan because it lets the steam escape and disrupts the cooking process. When cooking fish in a pan, I always tell the young chef I am working with to touch it, so they understand how it progressively goes from a dense sensation to a bouncier, lighter feel when it's done. Fish has a very short time from when it goes from succulent to dry.

Place a steamer big enough to hold your fish over medium-high heat. Once steam begins to form, lay a leaf (see Note) or a piece of parchment paper on the steamer basket, then gently lay the whole fish or fish fillet on top. Cover the pan and steam for 4 minutes.

With the lid on, turn the heat off and let it sit for an additional 2 minutes for fillets or 4 to 5 minutes for whole fish (the time varies depending on the fish). Before pulling the fish out of the steamer, ensure it is cooked through. Poke the thickest piece and pull it apart a little to make sure nothing is translucent and that everything is opaque. You can also touch it to make sure it's firm.

From here, you can serve it with many things: an herb yogurt, vinaigrette, oil, or beautiful seeds. You can flake it and maybe put it in an omelet. The possibilities are endless.

NOTE: Use an edible leaf when steaming to keep the underside of the fish protected and to help you remove the fish when it's done cooking. A large cabbage or collard leaf may be most accessible in some areas, and an avocado or fig tree leaf may be in others, and a banana, plantain, or coconut palm leaf in tropical climates. Look for edible leaves local to your area. While on the topic of leaves, they are great for grilling. I like covering the fish in leaves and tying it before I put it on the grill to prevent it from sticking, plus it cooks juicier because it's steaming within.

STEAMED PORGY WITH FRESH GINGER AND BLACK PEPPER UMAMI POWDER

Serves 2 to 4

This is my take on a classic Chinese steamed fish technique. Cooking a whole fish for a larger group is a joy for me because I love how you have to eat the fish delicately and share in the partaking. I recommend using chopsticks to dig out the little bits of fish and to avoid the bones carefully. Try to get a fish that fits comfortably in your largest frying pan with the lid on. You marinate the fish, then steam it with the marinade for a few minutes to end up with a super easy, fast, and—most importantly—very flavorful dish.

1½ to 2 lb [680 to 910 g] whole, gutted, scaled porgy
or similar fish, rinsed and dried

3 Tbsp julienned ginger

2 Tbsp rice wine or white wine

3 Tbsp sesame oil

1½ Tbsp soy sauce

2 green onions, thinly sliced

2 tsp Black Pepper Umami Powder (page 114)

In a shallow bowl that will fit in your steamer, place the fish along with the ginger, wine, 2 Tbsp of the sesame oil, and soy sauce. Cover and let marinate for 10 minutes at room temperature.

Set up the steamer over medium heat. Once steam forms, place the bowl with the fish in the steamer, cover, and steam for 5 minutes. With the lid on, turn off the heat and let it sit for an additional 4 minutes.

Carefully remove the bowl with the fish from the steamer and spoon the sauce from below over the fish. Finish with a drizzle of the remaining 1 Tbsp sesame oil, green onions, and umami powder and serve.

PHOTO-
GRAPHERS

GENTL & HYERS,
TARA SGROI,
S H A D I,
JONATHAN
BUMBLE,
AND CAMILLE
BECERRA

THANKS

PALOMA RIVERA,
REBECCA BARTOSHESKY,
HANNAH MILLMAN,
ELAINA SULLIVAN,
AYESHA PATEL,
FEISAL LAGOS,
ALIVIA BLOCH,
LUCINDA CONSTABLE,
NICOLE MESSINA,
CRISTINA GARCES,
MEG THOMPSON

RECIPE LIST

INDEX

Chronicle Books publishes distinctive books and gifts. From award-winning children's titles, bestselling cookbooks, and eclectic pop culture to acclaimed works of art and design, stationery, and journals, we craft publishing that's instantly recognizable for its spirit and creativity. Enjoy our publishing and become part of our community at www.chroniclebooks.com.